Never Such a Campaign

The Battle of Second Manassas, August 28–30, 1862

by Dan Welch and Kevin R. Pawlak

EMERGING CIVIL WAR SERIES

Chris Mackowski, series editor
Cecily Nelson Zander, chief historian

The Emerging Civil War Series

offers compelling, easy-to-read overviews of some of the Civil War's most important battles and stories.

Recipient of the Army Historical Foundation's Lieutenant General Richard G. Trefry Award for contributions to the literature on the history of the U.S. Army

Also part of the Emerging Civil War Series:

The Carnage was Fearful: The Battle of Cedar Mountain, August 9, 1862 by Michael Block

John Brown's Raid: Harpers Ferry and the Coming of the Civil War, October 16–18, 1859 by Jon-Erik Gilot and Kevin Pawlak

The Last Road North: A Guide to the Gettysburg Campaign, 1863 by Robert Orrison and Dan Welch

Race to the Potomac: Lee and Meade After Gettysburg, July 4–14, 1863 by Bradley M. and Linda I. Gottfried

Richmond Shall Not Be Given Up: The Seven Days' Battles, June 25–July 1, 1862 by Doug Crenshaw

Stay and Fight It Out: The Second Day at Gettysburg, July 2, 1863—Culp's Hill and the Northern End of the Battlefield by Kristopher D. White and Chris Mackowski

That Field of Blood: The Battle of Antietam, September 17, 1862 by Daniel J. Vermilya

To Hazard All: A Guide to the Maryland Campaign, 1862 by Robert Orrison and Kevin Pawlak

A Want of Vigilance: The Bristoe Station Campaign, October 9–19, 1863 by Bill Backus and Robert Orrison

For a complete list of titles, visit
https://www.savasbeatie.com/civil-war/emerging-civil-war-series/

Never Such a Campaign

The Battle of Second Manassas,
August 28–30, 1862

by Dan Welch and Kevin R. Pawlak

EMERGING CIVIL WAR SERIES

Savas Beatie
California

First edition, first printing

ISBN-13: 978-1-61121-641-7 (paperback)
ISBN-13: 978-1-61121-642-4 (ebook)

Library of Congress Cataloging-in-Publication Data

Names: Welch, Dan (Educator), author. | Pawlak, Kevin R., author.
Title: Never such a campaign : the Battle of Second Manassas, August
  28-August 30, 1862 / by Dan Welch and Kevin R. Pawlak.
Other titles: Battle of Second Manassas, August 28-August 30, 1862
Description: El Dorado Hills, CA : Savas Beatie, [2024] | Series: Emerging
  Civil War series | Includes bibliographical references. | Summary:
  "Historians Dan Welch and Kevin Pawlak follow Lee and Pope as they
  converge on ground once-bloodied just thirteen months earlier. Since
  then the armies had grown in size and efficiency, and combat between
  them would dwarf that first battle. For the second summer in a row,
  forces would clash on the plains of Manassas, and the results would be
  far more terrible"-- Provided by publisher.
Identifiers: LCCN 2023044022 | ISBN 9781611216417 (paperback) | ISBN
  9781611216424 (ebook)
Subjects: LCSH: Bull Run, 2nd Battle of, Va., 1862. |
  Virginia--History--Civil War, 1861-1865. | Pope, John, 1822-1892.
Classification: LCC E473.77 .W44 2023 | DDC 973.7/32--dc23/eng/20231002
LC record available at https://lccn.loc.gov/2023044022

Printed and bound in the United Kingdom

SB

Published by
Savas Beatie LLC
989 Governor Drive, Suite 102
El Dorado Hills, California 95762
916-941-6896
sales@savasbeatie.com
www.savasbeatie.com

Savas Beatie titles are available at special discounts for bulk purchases in the United States by corporations, institutions, and other organizations. For more details, e-mail us at sales@savasbeatie.com, or visit our website at www.savasbeatie.com for additional information.

For those who died for their country, and their old flag.

Table of Contents

List of Maps

Maps by Edward Alexander

Acknowledgments

We first wish to sincerely thank Ted Savas at Savas Beatie. Ted continues to be a leading publisher of works on the American Civil War, and this book could not have come into print without him. Chris Mackowski, co-founder at Emerging Civil War and the Emerging Civil War Series editor, deserves our sincerest thanks, as well. As editor, he has graciously guided us through the ups and downs of writing this book. Both Ted's and Chris's patience during the extended drafting of the manuscript will be a debt that can never be repaid (well, perhaps with a high-end cigar or two).

Many people kindly gave us their time to help make this book possible. Edward Alexander created the maps depicting numerous actions and movements during the Second Manassas campaign. Rob Orrison originally signed onto the project several years ago. Sadly for us, Rob left the project for an immersion into an earlier American conflict. You can find Rob's work over on the Emerging Revolutionary War blog (www.emergingrevolutionarywar.org), as co-author of several books in the Emerging Revolutionary War Series, and as chief historian of the ERW book series.

No one can write a book about this campaign or battle without a huge debt of gratitude to historian John Hennessy. Throughout the 1980s and 1990s, John's continued research, writing, and battlefield tours brought forth many new interpretations of the actions, primary sources that had not seen the light of day since their publication more than 100 years earlier, and clarity to some of the most complicated moments of the fighting. His in-depth map study and written narrative, and later, his campaign study, have left an indelible mark on the historiography of this period of the war in the Eastern Theater. John also offered his thoughts and comments on this manuscript and penned the foreword. There is no one else who has done more than John to entrench the importance and impact of the Second Manassas campaign into the historical consciousness, and we are honored to have his name in this book.

We would also like to thank our colleagues and friends in the field for agreeing to read through several drafts of the manuscript and provide insightful comments and suggestions. With each review they greatly assisted in making this not only a better manuscript, but the finished narrative history you have today. Of special note: Mark Maloy, Phill Greenwalt, and Billy Griffith. Thanks must also go to the staff at Manassas National Battlefield Park. Every day they continue to preserve and protect this hallowed ground, interpret those fateful events in August 1862, and bring long forgotten voices and lessons back into the public historical consciousness.

Though many people pushed this book across the finish line to the printers, any mistakes or errors are entirely our own.

Lastly, we could not have written this book without those, both North and South, who participated in and extensively wrote about their experiences in the Second Manassas campaign. It is to them that we dedicate this book. If it was not for their efforts to preserve and share what they saw, felt, and thought in August 1862, this book would have been impossible to write.

PHOTO CREDITS: Atlas of Hardin Co., Ohio: From Records & Original Surveys (aohc); Battles and Leaders of the Civil War (b&l); Chris Mackowski (cm); Civil War Medical Museum (cwmm); Dan Welch (dw); History of the 88th Pennsylvania Volunteers in the War for the Union, 1861-1865 (hopa); History of the Ninth Regiment N.Y.S.M. (honr); Kevin Pawlak (kp); Library of Congress (loc); Massachusetts in the War 1861–1865 (mitw); Military Order of the Loyal Legion of the United States (mollus); National Archives (na); New York State Military Museum (nysmm); The New England States, their Constitutional, Judicial, Educational, Commercial, Professional, and Industrial History (nes); *Our Soldier in the Civil War* (oscw); Personal Narratives of the Events in the War of the Rebellion (pn); Photographic History of the Civil War (phofcw); Tulane University (tu); U.S. Department of Agriculture (usda); Virginia Historical Society (vhs); *Western Pennsylvania Historical Magazine* (wphm); Wikipedia (wikip)

For the Emerging Civil War Series

Theodore P. Savas, *publisher*
Sarah Keeney, *editorial consultant*
Veronica Kane, *production supervisor*
Pat McCormick, *copyeditor*
David Snyder, *proofreader*

Chris Mackowski, *series editor and co-founder*
Cecily Nelson Zander, *chief historian*
Kristopher D. White, *emeritus editor*

Design and layout by Veronica Kane
Maps by Edward Alexander

𝓕oreword

BY JOHN J. HENNESSY

They say there have been more than 60,000 books written about the American Civil War; thousands have been written about Gettysburg alone. Only six volumes focus in any significant way on the Second Manassas campaign. Between 1881 and 1993, the nation suffered a 112-year stretch during which only one book (a rather insufferable one at that) appeared on the campaign.

Why the shade?

We like simplicities: beginnings and ends, climaxes and turning points. Second Manassas was none of these. Some see it as a bloody wayside on the armies' path from the Peninsula to Antietam Creek. Consequently, far too many have in their readings or explorations simply sped by with barely a glance. That's too bad.

In our insistence on simplicities, we also see Second Manassas as a mismatch: the polished and inevitable Lee against the toplofty and tetchy John Pope, interloper from the West. But in the summer of 1862, Lee was hardly polished and far from predestined. When he met Pope in central Virginia, Lee had been in command of his Army of Northern Virginia for only 25 days longer than Pope had command of his. While Pope did largely undo himself in the end, until that end on August 30, he posed a formidable challenge to Lee, and for much of the campaign matched him day-by-day.

Instead of abiding conventional wisdom or indulging simplicities—almost all of them incomplete or outright wrong—look at this and every campaign in

Two Napoleons mark the location of the 5th Maine Artillery Battery on Chinn Ridge. This location witnessed intense combat on August 30, 1862. (dw)

another way: what can it tell us about the war at large? Few campaigns tell us more about a war that by 1862 was in dramatic evolution than Second Manassas.

Second Manassas marks the emergence of the Army of Northern Virginia as we know it. The campaign might be the war's best example of outstanding maneuver within the theater (Jackson's flank march) and opportunistic, excellent tactical execution on the ground (Longstreet's August 30 attack), all within a matter of days. On no other battlefield of the war do we see Lee, Longstreet, and Jackson at the same time and in the same place fulfilling the roles that best suited them. Throw in Stuart's aggression with his cavalry (though still closely tied to Lee's infantry), and you have a case study in the high command of the Army of Northern Virginia. Never again would its most famous commanders perform so well in concert—and achieve such dramatic results.

No campaign of the Civil War better illustrates the challenges that faced an evolving Union war effort in 1862. In no campaign are the politics and practice of war more vividly intertwined. Pope was no political general, but politics had a great deal to do with his appointment to command. He was a counterweight to the more conservative, conciliatory McClellan, who had thus far dominated headlines in the East. Lincoln's attempt to use Pope to move the Union war effort beyond McClellan's reluctance to embrace emancipation as a war policy and his insistence on more conciliatory policies toward Southern civilians is drama itself. Interwoven as it was with the events at Manassas, the milieu of politics and the military reveals much about a war changing rapidly with each passing month.

And then there is this: Every battle has its internal dramas. Every battlefield has sites that for moments or minutes assumed such a significance that men were willing to die in the defense of or quest for them. At Manassas, as elsewhere, many are forgotten, but this book helps recall them. The fence lines on the Brawner and Dogan farms, where the Iron Brigade clashed with Jackson's men in the failing light of August 28. At Chinn Ridge, where a brigade of Ohioans fought furiously in a quest for nothing more tangible than time—time enough to allow others to do something more substantial. The men knew this and usually acted without hesitation, confident that even though they may not have understood the "why" of their assignment, their commanders did. At Manassas and elsewhere, men often hurled themselves into places or attempted to do things that in retrospect seem insane or awe inspiring—and sometimes both. It's not much to ask of us, today, to recall such events, such places, such sacrifices, such men.

Kevin Pawlak and Dan Welch help us do just that. This is not a scholarly analysis of the Second Manassas campaign, but a crisp and thoughtful narrative that draws deeply on primary sources and builds on work done by others. Kevin, who works in Prince William County's Office of Historic Preservation (much of the campaign played out in Prince William County), and Dan, a seasonal ranger at Gettysburg, are fine public historians. Their presentations are clear and fresh, and this book is, too. It, along with many others in the Emerging Civil War series, is just what the public needs; as Allan Nevins advised, books should reveal the product of an author's labors, not the labor itself.

We revel in the what-ifs of the war and spend far too little time considering its realities. Second Manassas was as decisive a tactical outcome as Lee achieved during the war—a stunning victory, nearly an existential moment for the Army of Northern Virginia. But through the lens of decades, we can now see that Lee's victory and Pope's defeat did not much move the needle toward ultimate victory or defeat. Indeed, when we look closely, no single battle really did—not Jackson's stunning successes in the Valley in 1862, Union disaster at Fredericksburg, Lee's unlikely triumph at Chancellorsville in 1863, or even Meade's triumph at Gettysburg or the fall of Vicksburg (which may lay the strongest claim to a "turning point"). The outcome of the Civil War turned on the cumulative effect of myriad campaigns, policies, elections, and the long-term presence of armies in the field. By the time the armies arrived on the fields of Manassas in August 1862, the war had become so large, so consumptive, and so complex, that no single battle would determine its outcome. Second Manassas is a vivid window on war expanding and changing, and Kevin Pawlak and Dan Welch have done the campaign, the battle, and the men who waged it noble justice in writing this book.

Historian JOHN J. HENNESSY *is the author of several books on Manassas, including* Return to Bull Run: The Campaign and Battle of Second Manassas.

Prologue

Thirteen months after the war's first major battle, war had once again descended on the plains of Manassas. Major General James Longstreet watched as thousands of Union troops withdrew from a major attack against "Stonewall" Jackson's line. Longstreet and army commander Robert E. Lee sensed the time had come for a counterstroke. Orders raced out from their headquarters for the attack to begin. Soon, tens of thousands of Confederates would surge forward, intent on destroying John Pope's Army of Virginia before the sun set on August 30, 1862.

Longstreet summoned Brig. Gen. John B. Hood to his headquarters. Longstreet understood a line of attack of this length, the number of units and men involved, and the terrain in front of them all required strict adherence to orders and coordination for it to be successful. Longstreet also understood his commanding officers, particularly Hood. He reminded Hood not to let himself or his division get caught up in the flush of victory and move too far forward without his supports to his rear and off to his right.

As Longstreet spoke to Hood, however, it was already too late. Parts of Hood's command had already "sprang to their work, and moved forward with all the steadiness and firmness that characterizes war-worn veterans."

Hood's Texas Brigade made the first contact with the enemy. Positioned opposite their front, the 1,100 soldiers of the 5th and 10th New York Infantry were not supposed to be there in the first place. Earlier in the afternoon, Lt. Charles E. Hazlett's Battery D, 5th

A modern view from the position of Charles Hazlett's battery on August 30. You can see the home of widow Lucinda Dogan and her five children at the time of the battle in the distance. It is the only remaining wartime structure of the small village of Groveton. (dw)

Like John Pope, John Bell Hood was a native Kentuckian and West Point graduate. Once joining the Confederate army in the spring of 1861, Hood time and again impressed his men and his commanding officers as a hard-fighting, tenacious, and determined leader of men. (loc)

At 24 years old, Louis A. Matos left home to enlist in the 5th New York Infantry. As a private in Co. C, he was captured during the fighting on August 30, 1862. Later paroled, he mustered out in May 1863. (loc)

U.S. Artillery had deployed on a knoll just south of the Warrenton Turnpike. The battery was originally supported by a division of Pennsylvania Reserves under the command of Brig. Gen. John F. Reynolds, but not long after the artillerists' deployment, Reynolds received orders to move east and abandon the knoll. Now with no infantry support, the lone battery was a tempting target for the assaulting Confederates.

The battery commander, Hazlett, rode to nearby brigade commander Col. Gouverneur K. Warren, to see "if he could not give me some support while I sent back word to General Porter of the state of affairs." Warren promptly ordered his two Zouave units—regiments that wore uniforms inspired by French colonial troops—to Hazlett's support. Only these units stood between Hood and Henry Hill, Longstreet's objective.

We "rushed forward at a charge from the word go, all the time keeping up an unearthly yell," a soldier in the 18th Georgia recalled. Arriving at a distance of less than 100 yards from Warren's main line, each side delivered devastating volleys of fire. The "steady well-directed aim of our Texas men told heavily on the enemy, and the carnage was terrible," a Texas soldier recorded. Private Andrew Coats in the 5th New York said, "For a short time the Regiment tried to fight back the overwhelming force that was pouring in a fearful stream of destruction and death upon it, but the stream became a torrent, as the right and left flanks of the enemy almost surrounded us." Of the carnage the Texas Brigade inflicted on the New Yorkers, Coats continued, "War has been designated as Hell, and I can assure you that where the Regiment stood that day was the very vortex of Hell. Not only were men wounded, or killed, but they were riddled."

Warren realized this was a fight that his small brigade could not win. He tried in vain to send orders down the line to begin a fighting retreat, but those orders either could not be heard over the cacophony of the battle or were not received. Finally, Warren made it to the color guard, and, by taking the flag and gesturing with it, was able to convey to the color-bearers to take the flags and color guard down the slope toward Young's Branch.

Private Alfred Davenport in the 5th New York remembered that neither he nor any of the men around him actually heard the order to retreat, but it was apparent that those orders had been given.

"The recruits began to give way & then the whole Regmt. broke & ran for their lives. The Rebels after us with their yells, meant to represent an Indian war whoop. . . ."

"While running down the hill toward the small stream at its foot," continued Davenport, "I saw the men dropping on all sides, canteens struck & flying to pieces, haversacks cut off, rifles knocked to pieces, it was a perfect hail of bullets. . . ."

Victory for Hood's Texans and Longstreet's attack seemed almost guaranteed. The path to Henry Hill now seemed open.

John Bendix enlisted in September 1861 as colonel of the 10th New York Infantry. He continued to lead the 10th through the end of his two year enlistment. (loc)

George M. Dewey mustered in as second lieutenant of Co. I, 10th New York Infantry in the wake of the fall of Fort Sumter. He led Co. F at Second Manassas until being wounded and captured on August 30. He received an on-field parole on September 2. Wounded in the Wilderness in May 1864, he was later discharged for disability that year. (loc)

"There never was such a campaign, not even by Napoleon."
— Brig. Gen. William Dorsey Pender

Glad to See You at Washington

CHAPTER ONE
JULY 1-25, 1862

"More than thirty thousand Confederate dead and wounded, the irreplaceable flower of a nation's early enthusiasm" littered the scarred landscape of the Virginia Peninsula by the early summer of 1862. The struggle to protect Richmond had raged in earnest since the early days of May, but now, two months later, Gen. Robert E. Lee and the Army of Northern Virginia could finally rest.

Lee had succeeded in commanding this army during a very tense campaign. Confederate forces had fallen back time and again, moving closer and closer to Richmond. Lee had to turn the campaign around, win tactical victories, and change the strategic situation on the Peninsula. In late June, he attacked the massive Federal army led by Maj. Gen. George B. McClellan. The resulting Seven Days Battles pushed McClellan's Army of the Potomac away from Richmond, saving the Confederate capital from Federal conquest.

At the beginning of July, Lee considered the military situation and his next step. He quickly arrived at two objectives that would dictate any strategy for the coming weeks and months. First, at all costs, Richmond must be protected from capture. Although he had pushed McClellan's army far down the Peninsula, it still loomed as a threat within a couple days' march of the Confederate capital. Second, Lee had witnessed over the previous months the abandonment of large portions of his native state. He believed he should utilize his army to recapture and

Much occurred in Washington, D.C., that ultimately shaped the Second Manassas campaign. From the decision to bring John Pope east, to the strictures placed on him to prosecute the campaign, and the formation of the Army of Virginia, all originated from a shaken nation's capital in the wake of Lee's victories on the Virginia peninsula. (loc)

General Robert E. Lee resigned his commission from the United States Army on the evening of April 19, 1861 and submitted it the following day. After a poor performance in West Virginia, and coastal defense duty in Georgia, Lee's second campaign as commander of the Army of Northern Virginia would be Second Manassas. (loc)

Major General George McClellan left for the Virginia Peninsula with the Army of the Potomac in April 1862. After a series of defeats and being pushed back down the peninsula, his army remained there until August 1862. (loc)

restore the state of Virginia to Confederate control. As historian Joseph Harsh noted, Lee realized "[t]here was no way to accomplish either goal save going on the strategic offensive." Lee set about achieving his objectives. His eyes returned to the 87,000-man army under McClellan at Harrison's Landing.

* * *

As these events played out on the Peninsula and in Richmond during June 1862, plans were in motion in Washington, D.C. to change the stalled strategic situation in Virginia. Lincoln and his advisors looked to create a new army in the state that would support McClellan and protect their own capital, and they needed a commander they could trust.

On June 19, a telegram arrived in St. Louis, Missouri, to the home of John Pope.

Major General John Pope's star had risen after several battlefield successes in the Western Theater. President Abraham Lincoln, members of his cabinet, and the United States War Department took notice. For them, Pope was the right man for the job at that time.

Pope was born into a prominent family in 1826 in Louisville, Kentucky, which allowed him to attend West Point, where he graduated seventeenth in the Class of 1842. A veteran of the Mexican-American War, following its conclusion he worked as a surveyor in Minnesota, demonstrated the navigability of the Red River, and served as the chief engineer of the Department of New Mexico from 1851 to 1853. His keen eye and skill in these roles continually earned him regular promotions, reaching the rank of captain in 1856. During the remainder of the antebellum years, Pope surveyed a route for the Pacific Railroad.

The secession winter of 1860–1861 found Pope serving on lighthouse duty. Incredibly ambitious and possessing an insatiable desire for promotion, he wrote a seven-page letter to newly elected President Abraham Lincoln offering advice on the state of the military at that time. Pope used the letter to get into Lincoln's inner circle and to get his name on any future list of promotions. Although he offered to serve Lincoln as an aide after the president's inauguration, he was instead appointed brigadier general of volunteers (date of rank effective May 17, 1861) and was ordered to Illinois to recruit men. His responsibilities grew as he ascended in the Federal army's command structure. Successful actions at Blackwater, Missouri,

LEFT: Major General John Pope arrived in Washington with much bluster in the summer of 1862. No one could have imagined that in just a matter of months he would be sent out to the Department of the Northwest in Minnesota with the defeat at Second Manassas still loudly ringing in his ears. (loc)

RIGHT: When Abraham Lincoln was elected, during his train ride to Washington John Pope served as an escort. Pope was well-known by the president when Lincoln summoned him to the nation's capitol in the summer of 1862. (loc)

in December 1861, and the capture of New Madrid and Island No. 10 in early 1862, were enough to prompt Lincoln to promote Pope to major general on March 21, 1862.

Three months later, Pope was home in St. Louis, visiting his wife Clara and their first-born child, Clara Horton, when on June 19 he received a telegram from Secretary of War Edwin Stanton. "If your orders will admit and you can be absent long enough from your command, I would be glad to see you at Washington," it read.

Pope, for once, had no ambitions either to go to Washington or to accept the promotion that might come as a result of his visit. Orders were orders, though, and Pope followed them unexcitedly. As he left for the train station, one observer said, "Good-bye Pope, your grave is made."

Pope arrived at the nation's capital on June 24, 1862, to an "enthusiastic welcome," reported the *Philadelphia Inquirer*. Since her husband had left, Clara wrote to him that she was "perfectly convinced" he

Island Number 10 on the Mississippi River held out for a month and a half against the joint efforts of the Federal army and navy. On April 8, 1862, the Confederate fortress fell, opening one more section of the river, but John Pope's important successful operation against the island was overshadowed by Ulysses S. Grant's nearly simultaneous victory at Shiloh—an event that stunned Americans because it resulted in more casualties than all other wars up to that point in the nation's history. (oscw)

Edwin Stanton's formative years were marked by loss and financial insecurity. Unable to finish college due to a lack of finances, it was an apprenticeship and the study of law that ultimately found a secure income and profession for him. As his notoriety grew within the law field, so too did his renown in politics. By the time of his confirmation as Secretary of War in January 1862 he was widely known and respected in many circles. (loc)

would not return to the West. "I am almost sure that you now will have Banks and Fremont's and perhaps McDowell's departments and that you will then take the field against Jackson," she penned. "It is possible that you may supersede McClellan, but I do not with my present light on the subject consider it likely." Her words were a presentiment of things to come.

The following day, Pope had his first interview with Secretary Stanton, although Stanton could not reveal to Pope why he had been ordered to Washington or any other details. The secretary remained tight-lipped as he awaited President Lincoln's arrival back at the White House from a strategy-defining trip to West Point to confer with Maj. Gen. Winfield Scott.

When Lincoln returned, Stanton revealed plans to create a new army with the objectives of protecting Washington, defending the Shenandoah Valley, and disrupting the Virginia Central Railroad near Charlottesville and Gordonsville. Stanton and Lincoln believed this threat would force Lee's Army of Northern Virginia from their strong positions around Richmond, allowing McClellan an easier second chance of taking it. Stanton also revealed to Pope that this was why he was called east, to carry out these objectives.

Following a long silence, Stanton turned to Pope. "General, you don't seem to approve the arrangements I have outlined to you."

"Mr. Secretary, I entirely concur in the wisdom of concentrating these widely scattered forces [Banks, Fremont, McDowell] in front of Washington and using them generally as you propose, but I do certainly not view with any favor the proposition to place me in command of them," Pope responded.

Pope had misgivings about the position. Asked why, he told Stanton that because the aforementioned generals outranked him, they would resent him. Furthermore, the men in the ranks might distrust him because he had been summoned from another theater of the conflict. Finally, he felt it would take far too much time to organize and discipline the disparate units into a new army. "In short, I should be much in the situation of the strange dog, without even the right to run out of the village," and placed in the command "of a forlorn hope under the most unfavorable conditions possible for success."

Stanton was unconvinced by Pope's reasons for not taking the command and agreed to refer the matter to Lincoln himself. The three men later met privately. The meeting concluded with the president's decision that Pope must stay in the East. On June 26, Maj. Gen. John Pope assumed command of the Army of Virginia.

Pope was next called to meet with Lincoln and his Cabinet regarding the situation of McClellan's army on the Peninsula. McClellan pleaded for reinforcements as he pulled back toward the James River, but Pope said McClellan's course of action was a mistake. Instead, Pope believed McClellan's army should be halted and allow time for Pope's new army to place the Confederate capital and the Army of Northern Virginia between the two commands. Pope continued by stating that if McClellan was not ordered to stop his withdrawal toward the James River, he would prefer to return to the West.

Lincoln would not hear of it. Pope was stuck in his new command in the Eastern Theater.

"I was compelled to undertake a duty hopeless of successful performance, except under the most favorable circumstances and the most genuine and zealous cooperation, both of which were conspicuously absent, as I strongly suspected would be the case at the time," wrote Pope. With no other recourse to evade his placement as commander, Pope assessed his new command, by telegraph and couriers, and worked to remedy its many ills.

Pope's new army comprised three corps, all of which had operated independently prior to the creation of the Army of Virginia. Commanding the I Corps was Maj. Gen. Franz Sigel, a darling of the German-American community in the North, with a reputation of unreliability as a military commander. Major General Nathaniel Banks commanded the II Corps. Although he had an impressive political resume, including the governorship of Massachusetts, his military experience paled in comparison. Just months earlier his command was roughly handled by Stonewall Jackson in the Valley, earning him the nickname "Commissary Banks" for supplies Jackson's men had captured. The last corps of Pope's new army was commanded by Maj. Gen. Irvin McDowell. Out of the three corps commanders Pope inherited, McDowell was his favorite, despite the lackluster reputation he had earned as a result of the battle of First Manassas.

German-born Franz Sigel attended a military academy there in his youth. He fled his country during political and military unrest, later settling in New York. A teacher in America, he was also active in New York's militia before the war. (loc)

LEFT: The "Bobbin Boy of Massachusetts," Nathaniel Banks, worked in a cotton mill during his youth and received very little education. Although he passed the bar at 23, his political rise was marked by numerous defeats. Yet, by 1861, he was governor of the state before Lincoln gave him a political military appointment to the rank of major general. (loc)

RIGHT: Irvin McDowell's humiliating defeat a year earlier on the plains of Manassas was a hard reputation to shake. His service in the field was renewed with an appointment by Lincoln to major general and assignment to command a corps in McClellan's Army of the Potomac. He was then transferred to command a corps in Pope's Army of Virginia upon its creation. (loc)

In all, the Army of Virginia numbered approximately 51,000 men, but this number was beset by a host of problems that belied their numerical strength. The new army's combat readiness remained highly suspect due to the exertions and defeats of its constituent parts during the previous spring campaigns. It suffered from low morale, a lack of supplies, desertions, and officer absences. As Pope issued orders from a distance in Washington, D.C., they were largely ignored, and every deadline Pope included in those orders was missed. The responses Pope did receive from his subordinates often asked for secure lines of retreat to be established before they would move their individual commands. Fed up with his subordinates thus far, on July 14, Pope issued the following to the Army of Virginia:

Let us understand each other. I have come to you from the West, where we have always seen the backs of our enemies; from an army whose business it has been to seek the adversary and to beat him when he was found; whose policy has been attack and not defense. . . . I presume that I have been called here to pursue the same system and to lead you against the enemy. It is my purpose to do so, and that speedily. I am sure you long for an opportunity to win the distinction you are capable of achieving. That opportunity I shall endeavor to give you. Meantime I desire you to dismiss from your minds certain phrases, which I am sorry to find so much in vogue amongst you. I hear constantly of "taking strong positions and holding them," of "lines of retreat," and of "bases of supplies." Let us discard such ideas. . . . Let us study the probable lines of retreat of our opponents, and leave our own to take care of themselves. Let us look before us, and not behind. Success and glory are in the advance, disaster and shame lurk in the rear. Let us act on this understanding, and it is safe to predict that your banners shall be inscribed with many a glorious deed and that your names will be dear to your countrymen forever.

Reviews of his message were mixed across the Federal armies and high command. Fitz John Porter, a corps commander in the Army of the Potomac, wrote to J. C. G. Kennedy, chief of the Census Bureau, three days later, "I regret to see that General Pope has not improved since his youth and has now written himself down as what the military world has long known, an ass. His address to his troops will make him ridiculous in the eyes of military men abroad as well [as] at home."

Although such a reaction could be expected from a high-ranking officer in the Army of the Potomac—which Pope's messaging subtly targeted—many enlisted men in the Army of Virginia welcomed his thoughts. One Ohio officer said of it, "The army is enthusiastic in its praises and adorations of our commanding general. He is the man for the times, a man who comprehends the wants of the loyal North, the magnitude and nature of this rebellion, and the best and most speedy way to crush it."

Pope's proclamation was only the beginning of a series of orders meant to place his army on the offensive in the coming campaign. On July 18, he issued General Order No. 5, which instructed his army to subsist off the land during their time in Virginia. The new order ended the practice found in the Army of the Potomac, as well as the commands that now formed the Army of Virginia, of protecting private dwellings and property.

Pope next issued General Order No.7, an order to hold the local citizenry accountable while the Army of Virginia operated in their area. Civilians were now to be held responsible for any destruction they committed to railroad tracks, railroad lines, roads, or any attacks they made on Federal trains or straggling Federal soldiers.

The last order issued in this flurry was General Order No. 11. It ordered the arrests of all disloyal male citizens within army lines. If they were unwilling to take the oath of allegiance they were to be sent farther south. If they were caught again within army lines, they would be considered spies and ordered to be hung. If they took the oath and violated any part of it, their property would be seized and they would be shot.

The orders Pope issued were a reversal of McClellan's approach to prosecuting the war when his army operated in Virginia. But were they out of place for this moment in the war? John Hennessy, a noted historian of this campaign and subsequent battle, argues that the orders "were not a dramatic reversal; they were a step away from conciliation."

Further research over the decades has revealed that Pope may not have written or directed these orders by himself; some historians argue that Secretary of War Stanton may have partially written the proclamation and the subsequent general orders, while President Lincoln approved them before Pope issued them. Pope's orders were then quickly followed by Lincoln's July 22 executive order instructing all Federal armies to operate similarly.

These orders demonstrated that the new commander of the Army of Virginia could be used as a political weapon by the Lincoln administration—a weapon that could perhaps spur McClellan into action or justify his removal, and be used as an argument against the conservative approach to war that was used in the Eastern Theater for the previous twelve months.

During all the political intrigue and drama that these orders created over much of July, the Army of Virginia plodded southward, deeper into Virginia.

*   *   *

Despite the bombast of Pope's proclamation and General Orders No. 5 and 7, Pope's army initially weighed little in Robert E. Lee's strategic plans and actions on the Virginia Peninsula. Eventually, however, Pope's army moved far enough into the Old Dominion to be within striking distance of a vital, strategic point on the Confederate supply line. Lee could no longer ignore Pope's army and had to change the strategic objectives he had committed to in the immediate aftermath of the Seven Days' Battles. Two Federal armies were now a threat to Richmond and his army—Pope's from the north and McClellan's from the south. If they cooperated, Lee would be forced to choose between abandoning Richmond

"Stonewall" Jackson's stunning victories in the Shenandoah Valley in the spring of 1862 allowed Lee to bring him and his army to the defense of Richmond that summer. His performance there was lackluster at best, but his opportunity to change course for more military laurels would lie in the Second Manassas campaign. (loc)

altogether or defending the capital and being caught in a classic military pincer movement.

Two days after Pope issued General Order No. 11, on July 25, Lee finally wrote to Thomas Jonathan "Stonewall" Jackson. Jackson, with 24,000 men, had been operating in Louisa County northwest of Richmond for nearly two weeks. In his note, Lee discussed the possibility of Jackson striking quickly at Pope, removing him from the strategic situation in Virginia, then returning to Lee outside the capital.

This was the first time Lee expressed any intention of offensive action against the Army of Virginia and his desire "to suppress Pope." Over the next several days, plans for both armies emerged as Lee and Pope made decisions that ultimately led to the plains of Manassas.

The Plan of Operations

CHAPTER TWO

JULY 27–AUGUST 19, 1862

Just two days after Lee wrote to Jackson discussing the challenges and possibilities of striking after Pope, Lee nonetheless decided on a strike as his next course of action, with Jackson at the helm.

On July 27, Lee ordered A. P. Hill's division to join Jackson at Gordonsville, which swelled the size of Jackson's command to approximately 36,000 men. Lee sought "to keep General McClellan quiet" until Jackson attacked and defeated Pope before returning to Lee's main body.

Like Lee with Jackson's command, Pope was not at the front with his army, either. Since taking command of the Army of Virginia, Pope had remained in Washington, D.C. Finally, on July 29, he caught up with his men. Now in the field, his orders from D.C. severely limited his operational abilities. He was to cover the capital from any enemy advance and, in the event of one, to delay it until the Army of the Potomac could arrive. His orders also covered the eventuality of Lee's army not moving at all. If Lee failed to budge, Pope was to entice action out of Lee by operating on his line of communications at Gordonsville and Charlottesville. These actions would force large detachments from Lee's army or the entirety of his command to move away from Richmond. Then, McClellan could successfully divest his army from the Peninsula without molestation by Lee.

Regardless of the burdens placed upon him, Pope continued to move his army southward toward a

Two silent cannons rest on the Cedar Mountain battlefield. In the distance sits the mountain itself. "Stonewall" Jackson's tactical victory here on August 9, 1862 was hollow at best. (dw)

A. P. Hill's star was on the rise since receiving the colonelcy of the 13th Virginia Infantry in the spring of 1861. In under a year, he rose to the rank of major general, displaying particularly strong leadership qualities during the Seven Days' battles. (loc)

Cedar Mountain was anything but a signal victory for Jackson and his command. The battle was sloppily fought, and although Pope's forces left the field, Jackson had not met Lee's expectations for his first engagement with the Army of Virginia. (b&l)

strong position on the Rapidan River. It was not long after the Army of Virginia settled into this area that "Stonewall" Jackson and Robert E. Lee looked for ways to get at the "miscreant" Pope and suppress him once and for all.

Still under orders from Lee to quickly attack Pope and return to the Army of Northern Virginia, Jackson did not immediately move against Pope, much to Lee's chagrin. Jackson could simply not find a way to get at Pope without costly frontal assaults north of the Rapidan and Lee agreed with Jackson's tactical assessment.

The situation on Jackson's front changed rapidly, however, and the promise of suppressing Pope looked better by August 7. By the next day, Jackson had learned that the Army of Virginia was moving to concentrate at Culpeper, albeit slowly. "Stonewall" believed he could attack a large portion of Pope's command as it sluggishly came into Culpeper and thus cripple Pope's ability to pose a threat for some time. Lee wholeheartedly backed Jackson's plan and ordered more of his army northward to Jackson's support if he needed it.

As soon as Jackson crossed the Rapidan River, alert Federal scouts notified headquarters. Pope surmised that his opponent was moving toward a concentration point at Culpeper and ordered his own army to concentrate there. What resulted on August 9, 1862, set against a backdrop of intense heat, was the battle of Cedar Mountain.

Jackson's men held the field at the end of that evening, but his tactical victory was hollow and costly. Still, it was a crushing blow to the newly created Army of Virginia.

As Jackson pulled his wing back south of the Rapidan River, morale in the Army of Virginia plummeted. Just months earlier, during the spring, the individual corps that composed Pope's army—once their own independent armies—had each received devastating blows at the hands of Jackson in the Shenandoah Valley, so this latest loss stirred recent bitter memories. While Pope's men marched away from the battlefield, widespread feelings of despair and frustration with the higher command rippled through the rank and file.

Worse, shortages of provisions for Pope's men accumulated. Now, weeks later, the army was in a dire state.

*   *   *

While Pope's army trudged northward, eventually crossing the Rappahannock River within a week of the battle of Cedar Mountain, Lee moved to once and for all break the strategic stalemate in Virginia.

Lee grew restless on the Peninsula while his army sat in a defensive posture. However, his keen strategic eye helped him better understand the Federal armies' operations and intent. Recent intelligence told Lee that McClellan's army was breaking its camps, and he correctly assumed they were doing so to join Pope's army. This left the Peninsula almost void of Federal activity and Pope isolated and alone. To break the deadlock across the state—with Pope along the Rappahannock, McClellan leaving Harrison's Landing, and Burnside at Fredericksburg—Lee seized upon the chance to regain the initiative in the Eastern Theater.

On August 13, he ordered Maj. Gen. James Longstreet to get his command ready for active campaigning. Longstreet's wing utilized the Virginia Central Railroad to head toward the developing situation around the Rappahannock River and Gordonsville.

The following day, Longstreet sent a dispatch to Lee suggesting an attack on Pope's right flank. The dispatch itself has been lost but, in his response, Lee offered the same counsel to Longstreet that Lee had given Jackson. "It is important that our movement, in whatever direction it is determined, should be as quick as possible," Lee wrote. "I fear General Pope can be re-enforced quicker than ourselves."

James Longstreet graduated in the same class at West Point as Army of Virginia commander John Pope. His bulldog fighting personality won him two brevets for gallantry in Mexico. By the time of the Second Manassas campaign, Longstreet commanded a wing of Lee's Army of Northern Virginia with the rank of major general. (loc)

Photographer Timothy O'Sullivan accompanied Pope's army during the Second Manassas Campaign. When Pope withdrew behind the Rappahannock River, fugitive slaves joined his northward withdrawal. O'Sullivan's camera captured their quest for freedom just downstream from the Rappahannock River railroad bridge, seen in the background. (loc)

As the focus of both armies shifted north, Lee decided to leave for the front on August 17 and have a conference with both of his wing commanders upon his arrival. He would not leave, however, until he felt the Richmond defenses were complete and ready to receive an attack while he was away on this new front.

Lee arrived on the 17th and set up his headquarters in the shadow of Clark's Mountain in Orange County. As was his nature, he set to work early on the morning of August 18. The Army of Virginia had positioned itself within a "V"-shaped piece of ground between the Rapidan and Rappahannock rivers. He determined to strike at Pope's left flank.

Lee needed his cavalry to move against Pope. His plan was to send the Confederate cavalry toward the Federal rear to burn the bridge at Rappahannock Station. As events transpired, however, Lee was forced to delay the army's attack until August 20.

Unfortunately, this delay was not clearly communicated to Maj. Gen. J. E. B. Stuart, recently promoted to command the Army of Northern Virginia's cavalry. The gray cavalier expected the arrival of a brigade of cavalry under the command of Brig. Gen. Fitzhugh Lee from Beaver Dam Station, and so set up his headquarters with his staff in Verdiersville.

When Stuart and the rest of his staff arrived at Verdiersville late on the evening of August 17, Lee's brigade had yet to arrive. Surprised, Stuart immediately ordered one of his staff officers to search for Lee's cavalry. That officer was later captured during his search.

The following morning, not knowing that Lee's brigade still had not arrived in the vicinity, Stuart sat blindly, eagerly listening for their arrival. "About four A.M. we heard the heavy trampling of a long column and the rumbling of artillery," Prussian aide Heros von Borcke wrote. Stuart's ears perked up as the sounds of a sizable cavalry force grew louder, a sure sign that Fitz Lee had arrived. Stuart was heard to quip in the moment, "Here comes Lee now." Under that impression, Stuart sent scout John S. Mosby and another courier to halt the column and have its commanding officer report to Stuart immediately. "A few seconds later we heard pistol-shots in rapid succession, and saw our two men come running towards us at a full run," remembered Von Borcke. The growing cacophony of 1,000 troopers riding down the road, however, did not come from Fitz Lee's brigade. Federal cavalry now raced toward the rest of Stuart's staff and their commander. Stuart hurried into his saddle, foregoing the extra time to grab his favorite hat and haversack, and hopped the garden fence into an open field while more Federal troops poured into the village. The company of Federal cavalry chased after the fleeing Confederates.

Many of Stuart's staff and Stuart himself gathered after the pursuers gave up their chase. Von Borcke could not help but stare at the "bareheaded" general as he "look[ed] at the disappearing column of the enemy, who were carrying off in triumph his beautiful hat . . . and his haversack, containing some important maps and documents." The story of Stuart's lost hat quickly spread through the ranks. Far more concerning was the loss of his haversack, however, for inside it contained orders from Lee describing the overall Confederate plan to attack the Army of Virginia.

The need to cancel the attack of August 18, coupled with the loss of Stuart's haversack and the dispatches inside it, were devastating blows to Lee's intentions for a quick victory against the Army of Virginia. Furthermore, Lee's intent to cross the Rapidan the following day, August 19, was also scrubbed. Due to the condition of the horses and

Major General James Ewell Brown "Jeb" Stuart was already a military celebrity across the North and South by the time of the Second Manassas campaign. He had already assisted Lee in the capture of John Brown in 1859, fought gallantly at First Manassas in July 1861, and ridden around McClellan and the Army of the Potomac before the Seven Days' battles. (loc)

Fitzhugh Lee was a nephew of General Lee and a native of Fairfax County, Virginia. He played critical parts in numerous campaigns and battles as part of Stuart's cavalry corps. (loc)

Born into Pomeranian nobility, Heros von Borcke emigrated to the Confederate States in 1862 after substantial financial setbacks. With prior Prussian cavalry experience, Von Borcke and his large Solingen straight sword were assigned to Stuart's cavalry. (loc)

men in part of Stuart's command, they would not be able to cross until the day after, August 20. The same situation played out in the infantry ranks: both wings needed to be provisioned before they resumed active operations. "The delay proved fatal to our success," Lee told President Jefferson Davis.

Little did Lee know that Pope had received critical intelligence from the affair at Verdiersville. With more Confederate forces massing against him and with the new intelligence captured from Stuart, Pope now understood that his army was the primary target of Lee and the Army of Northern Virginia. He ordered his army to pull back to the northern bank of the Rappahannock River. General-in-Chief Henry W. Halleck, Pope's old commander out west—and now in his new role in the east as commander of all Federal armies—agreed. "I fully approve your move," Halleck wrote on August 18. "Stand firm on that line until I can help you. Fight hard, and aid will soon come." Telegraphers in the War Department in Washington were about to have a busy day.

Upon receipt of Halleck's message, Pope sent a flurry of orders to his subordinates—where to provision the men, lines of march, points of concentration, and more—to strengthen his new line. At the same time, Halleck worked the telegraph lines from his end, trying to hold to his promise of getting plenty of reinforcements from the Army of the Potomac and Burnside's command to Pope as quickly as possible.

Over the next several days, Pope worked toward getting all his army north of the Rappahannock River and to prepare defensible positions at its numerous crossing points, but still no reinforcements arrived to assist in supporting his main line. In addition to a lack of promised support, Pope was also not happy with his position, which was based solely on receiving reinforcements. "The line of the Rappahannock offers no advantage for defense," Pope wrote to Halleck on August 20, "But I presume my position here is regulated by the arrival of McClellan's forces on the Lower Rappahannock."

Those forces had still not arrived when the situation worsened for Pope the following day. After intelligence poured into his headquarters at Rappahannock Station all day, Pope wired Halleck that evening, "The enemy are massing heavily upon our front and right, and everything indicates an assault upon our position to-morrow morning. We are all ready, and shall make the best fight we can." Only an hour before midnight, Halleck wired back to Pope that he would be on his own if his prediction was true. "Dispute every inch of ground, and fight like the devil, till we can reinforce you," Halleck advised. "Forty-eight hours more and we can make you strong enough. Don't yield an inch if you can help it."

A runaway in his youth, Henry Halleck later attended Hudson Academy, Union College, and West Point. His prewar résumé in the field of military theory and his real-world experience was extensive. Early war successes catapulted his notoriety, but his summons east paralyzed him from further battlefield exploits. (loc)

Pope's Best Coat

CHAPTER THREE

AUGUST 19-24, 1862

Upon seeing Pope's army retreating on August 19, Lee said to Longstreet, "General, we little thought that the enemy would turn his back upon us this early in the campaign." Now, with the Army of Virginia north of the Rappahannock River, and having "strongly guarded" the fords across it, Lee had no interest in attacking. The initial plan against Pope's left—the plan Jackson, Longstreet, and Stuart worked to achieve—was no longer viable with Pope in his new position. Lee instead began to look upriver above Pope's right flank for an opportunity to dislodge Pope from behind the river.

On August 20, the Army of Northern Virginia was back on the move. Crossing the Rapidan and continuing to march throughout the remainder of the hot August day, Lee's army had little to show for their efforts other than a better idea of Pope's new position from Kelly's Ford to Rappahannock Station.

The following day, to prepare for an attack on Pope's right, Lee ordered a crossing of the Rappahannock by a portion of Stuart's cavalry and Jackson's command at Beverly's Ford, just two miles north of Rappahannock Station. Jackson's gunners enthusiastically accepted their orders, starting an artillery duel that lasted much of the day. A Confederate cavalry foray across Beverly's Ford failed to accomplish much of anything.

By the morning of August 22, Jackson still searched for an unguarded or lightly defended crossing point

A modern railroad bridge stands near the same site of the wartime bridge over Cedar Run that Stuart's cavalrymen failed to burn on August 22, 1862. (kp)

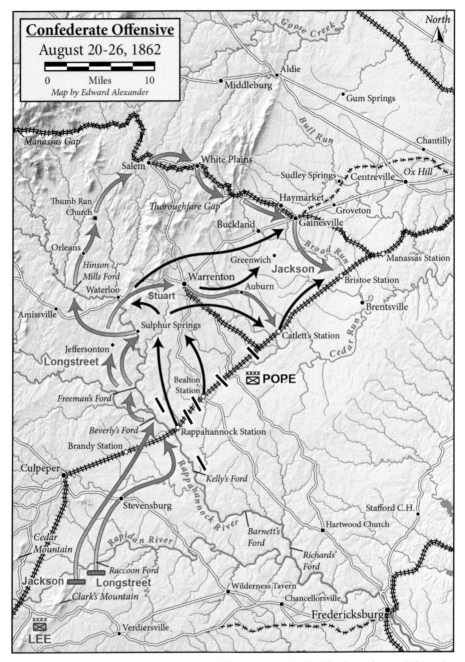

CONFEDERATE OFFENSIVE—After John Pope pulled his army back behind the Rappahannock River, he parried several attempts by Robert E. Lee to cross that river. Ultimately, Lee sent half of his army under "Stonewall" Jackson on a wide sweeping march around Pope's right flank.

Once General Pope realized Lee's point of attack, he ordered his army to pull back to the northern bank of the Rappahannock River, a scene depicted here. (b&l)

over the Rappahannock River. Marching northward from Beverly's Ford to Freeman's Ford, Jackson found it defended by portions of Franz Sigel's corps, which forced Jackson to continue his march further upriver to Sulphur Springs in Fauquier County. With Jackson's column in motion—a vulnerable time for any sized unit on the march—Sigel ordered an attack on the rear of Jackson's column at Freeman's Ford. The cost was extremely high to the Federals because they didn't just find teamsters and wagons—they ran into Confederate infantry, too, which counterattacked. Following the exchange, one Confederate soldier later recalled that the Rappahannock was "filled with the dead, wounded and dying" Federals. All were "floating downstream, almost covering its surface," the Confederate wrote.

When Jackson's column finally reached Sulphur Springs, it found the crossing there undefended; however, the bridge across the river had been burned two days earlier. It did not deter Jackson's resolve. He ordered Brig. Gen. Alexander Lawton's brigade and two batteries of artillery to cross at the Springs proper while he sent Brig. Gen. Jubal Early's brigade and Col. Henry Forno's brigade further downstream to cross at a dam.

Daylight and weather were against them. Jackson's crossing did not begin until after 5 p.m. and proceeded under heavy rain. By the time Early's brigade finished crossing, it was dark, and Jackson held Forno's brigade and the remainder of Lawton's brigade from crossing until morning. In the intervening hours, a heavy rainstorm rose the Rappahannock River six feet, isolating a small but important portion of Jackson's command. Jackson immediately ordered artillery down to the western bank of the river to cover Early's and Lawton's men from the opposite bank on the

Native South Carolinian, and West Point and Harvard graduate, Alexander Lawton gained an early war victory and acclaim in capturing Fort Pulaski in Georgia just days into 1861. He was a steady officer in the Army of Northern Virginia until his severe wounding at Antietam in September 1862. (loc)

Although a Virginia native, Jubal Early voted against secession by his state at its convention in April 1861. Despite his skepticism about secession, Early entered service in the Confederate army as colonel of the 24th Virginia Infantry, after which he quickly rose through the ranks. (loc)

morning of August 23. In addition, he sent orders to the engineers to construct a bridge as quickly as possible. Even Jackson himself was there to supervise, riding his horse into the Rappahannock. One witness noted of Jackson, "He was obviously suffering from intense anxiety."

Sensing an opportunity, Pope wrote to General Kearny that he was "moving his whole force . . . on Sulphur Springs," and expected "to be there to-night." He asked Kearny to forward support. General Sigel, who led Pope's advance, marched cautiously. Once at the Springs, and near the position of Early's and Lawton's small defense, only small Federal probes went forward.

Early's and Lawton's men could have been easily removed from the Confederate equation, their backs against an unfordable river; yet, once again, Jackson escaped. Daylight wasted away and, by darkness, with the bridge completed, the stranded Confederates re-crossed to safety on the western bank. In the early morning hours of August 24, after nearly 30 hours of being cut off by the Rappahannock River, the units were once again reunited with Jackson's army.

*   *   *

As Jackson's wing marched toward Sulphur Springs on August 22, General Lee approved a bold and daring strike at Pope's rear and his communications. Stuart, who proposed the idea, set out shortly after 10 a.m. and wasted no time getting his 2,000 men across the Rappahannock River at Waterloo Bridge and Hart's Ford, leaving only the 3rd and 7th Virginia Cavalry behind. While the column inched closer toward their goal of Catlett's Station on the Orange and Alexandria Railroad, a storm broke across the horizon—the same storm that cut off Early's and Lawton's commands. The fords that Stuart's men had crossed earlier in the day now flooded, blocking their return. The roads turned to quagmires, slowing down the cavalry, especially the horse artillery. As darkness fell on August 22, the gray cavaliers finally arrived in the vicinity of Catlett's Station around 8 p.m.

Stuart's decision to raid Catlett's Station was both strategic and personal. The railroad bridge over Cedar Run stood nearby. Its destruction would create chaos and logistical nightmares for Pope. Second, Pope's headquarters trains were at the station. Stuart saw an opportunity to avenge the loss of his hat and papers.

The first task for Stuart's men was to silence the Federal pickets. Heros von Borcke remembered that this was done with ease. Stuart and his men now moved closer to the station. They formed their lines approximately 200 hundred yards opposite the Federals when, against the wondrous cacophony of a stormy summer night, "Stuart nodded to his bugler: 'Sound the charge, Freed.'"

"The sound of a single trumpet was the signal for nearly 2000 horsemen to dash," remembered a rider in the charge, and "as they did with loud shouts, upon the utterly paralysed Yankees, who were cut down and made prisoners before they had recovered from their first astonishment." Von Borcke was now sent "to proceed with a select body of men to General Pope's tent." He and his men did not find Pope but were able to capture one of his uniforms, several pieces of official army correspondence, and some of his personal horses. Von Borcke even made off with a "magnificent field-glass" for himself.

While Von Borcke and his men rummaged through Pope's headquarters, a separate body of men composed of troopers from the 1st and 5th Virginia Cavalry and Capt. W. W. Blackford of the engineers

A modern image of the train tracks and buildings at Catlett's Station. (dw)

Famed Civil War sketch artist Alfred Waud produced this view of Catlett's Station in November 1862. (loc)

"attempted the destruction of the railroad bridge over Cedar Run." The hours of rain, coupled with the blowing wind, simply would not allow the bridge to be fired. The men then turned to axes to accomplish their mission. This too failed as there were too few axes on hand and the mighty timbers supporting the bridge would not yield to brute strength alone. Despite the overwhelming odds, these men continued their efforts to take the bridge down until growing musketry fire from across the bank drove them from their task.

By now, the surprise of the attack had worn off. Stuart's troopers were wildly disorganized after this nighttime of attacking, plundering, and pillaging. Many of the Federals that had retreated across the Cedar Run bridge reorganized and, with more reinforcements, "commenced a vigorous fire upon our men" from across the river. The scene that now presented itself was one of unimaginable chaos and confusion. Fires burned in all directions as far as the eye could see, the Confederate cavalry igniting wagons, depot buildings, and anything else they could set to flame amidst the rain.

Unable to destroy Cedar Run bridge, facing a decreasing ability to retain command and control, and knowing he needed to be far removed from the area by dawn, Stuart ordered his men to withdraw. The "great object of the expedition . . . the destruction of the Cedar Run railroad bridge," was left unaccomplished, Stuart wrote.

The work of Stuart's men did produce other victories. In addition to the capture of Pope's uniform coat and important Federal army correspondence, the raid netted numerous prisoners, hundreds of horses and mules, and even a payroll chest laden with thousands of dollars. Yet it was Pope's coat that Stuart prized most. Sending a note through the lines to the Federal commander, the cavalryman not only took a moment to gloat over his exploit but to also propose a trade. "You have my hat and plume. I have your best coat. I have the honor to propose a cartel for a fair exchange of the prisoners," Stuart wrote. Pope never officially responded.

By 2 a.m. the following morning, August 23, news of the raid reached Pope, who alerted Halleck to "some considerable damage." More importantly, however, the raid alerted Pope to the reality that his rear was vulnerable, including his railroad supply line and communications, both of which "may be unsafe

for a few days." Now, more than ever, he needed the reinforcements that had been promised to him more than two weeks earlier. He asked Halleck to forward troops from Warrenton Junction and Fredericksburg at all haste, along with further supplies. Nowhere did Pope share the news of his dress jacket.

This railroad bridge spanned Cedar Run not far from Catlett's Station. Although it survived the Second Manassas campaign, it was destroyed a year later during the Bristoe Station campaign. It was depicted contemporaneously by Alfred Waud. (loc)

* * *

From his headquarters near Brandy Station, Lee learned of Stuart's success at Catlett's Station. Stuart also wasted no time in showing off Pope's captured uniform, above all to both Lee and Jackson. It was the most levity Lee's headquarters saw that day.

Back to the business of war, later on August 23, Lee sat down to inform Richmond of the recent events and reveal his intent to continue operations in northern Virginia. That was not necessarily a challenge for Lee and his army, but it did require a massive commitment of troops from the Richmond defenses. Getting

Edwin Forbes sketched this artillery duel between Union and Confederate artillery on August 23, 1862 at Rappahannock Station. The sketch also depicts Federal infantry support for the batteries and Longstreet's troops on the march. (loc)

support for sending those reinforcements from the Confederate capital was Lee's challenge.

Lee suggested a change in the theater of war in Virginia, from Richmond to the state's northern borders. His writing eased the minds of those in the capital, including Davis, of stripping the city's defenses in favor of returning vast tracts of Virginia back to Confederate control, and a steady supply of provisions that could provide relief to the commissary department in the capital. As always, however, Lee told Davis to countermand any order of his that he did not agree with, and that he always remained Davis's "obedient servant." No countermand came.

The campaign progressed quickly now. On Sunday, August 24, Lee again met with Stuart and then Lee and his staff rode toward Jeffersonton, where he established new headquarters. There, Lee sat down to write to President Davis again. Now closer to the front, Lee described the position of Pope's army and estimated its strength at approximately 45,000— intelligence that Pope's captured papers revealed. "The enemy is in force before us," Lee wrote, "occupying the left bank of the Rappahannock." Concluding that McClellan's Army of the Potomac would join Pope's command any day, the Confederate commander felt "The whole army . . . should be united here as soon as possible."

It was also at his headquarters near Jeffersonton that Lee sent for General Jackson, who had also established his headquarters in the area. Noted southern historian Douglas Southall Freeman concluded it was a meeting between just the two men, yet several other contemporary accounts of this meeting, including one by Henry Kyd Douglas, an aide to Jackson, also placed generals Longstreet and Stuart in attendance. Regardless of the headcount, Freeman believed, "The conference that followed . . . was one of the most important Lee ever held."

Dr. Hunter McGuire, a medical officer on Jackson's staff, in 1897 wrote a letter to British military historian G. F. R. Henderson describing the events that took place at the August 24 meeting:

Hunter McGuire's familial profession of medicine took him into the field as well. Initially joining the 2nd Virginia Infantry as a private, his knowledge and experience in the medical field was quickly recognized. Promoted to brigade surgeon, he rose through the ranks and would be the surgeon that amputated Ewell's leg after his wounding on August 28. (cwmm)

The day before we started to march round Pope's army I saw Lee and Jackson conferring together. Jackson— for him—was very much excited, drawing with the toe of his boot a map in the sand, and gesticulating in a much more earnest way than he was in the habit of doing. General Lee was simply listening, and after Jackson had got through, he nodded his head, as if acceding to some proposal. I believe, from what occurred afterwards, that Jackson suggested the movement as it was made, but I have no further proof than the incident I have just mentioned.

Although no record exists of what was said during the conference, particularly of who proposed the movement toward Pope's rear, both Lee and Jackson in their official reports of the campaign mentioned its outcomes, albeit with brevity. Of the decisions made for Jackson and his command, Lee wrote: "In pursuance of the plan of operations determined upon, Jackson was directed on the 25th to cross above Waterloo and move around the enemy's right, so as to strike the Orange and Alexandria Railroad in his rear." Jackson's recollection, although it mostly mirrored Lee's, included more specificity to his role operating in Pope's rear: "Pursuing the instructions of the commanding general, I left Jeffersonton on the morning of the 25th to throw my command between Washington City and the army of General Pope and to break up his railroad communications with the Federal capital." According to these recollections, the next step in the campaign was purely another raid behind Pope's rear, and, if anything, an extension of what Stuart had done at Catlett's Station.

At the conclusion of the August 24 meeting with Lee, Jackson promised to ready his command immediately for its important march. "I will be moving within an hour," the general said, before turning to the task at hand. Only time would tell if Lee's gamble would pay off.

Such Troops as These

CHAPTER FOUR

AUGUST 25-26, 1862

Darkness and secrecy cloaked the purpose of the bugle calls that roused Jackson's foot cavalry from their bivouac at 3 a.m. on August 25. After a hasty preparation of their rations and the issuing of ammunition, Jackson's soldiers stepped into their lines. Officers yelled the day's orders: "No straggling; every man must keep his place in ranks; in crossing streams officers are to see that no delay is occasioned by removing shoes or clothing." Haste was necessary.

Captain James Boswell led the column and was one of the few men who knew its ultimate destination. Boswell initially turned Jackson's 24,000 men in the direction of the Shenandoah Valley before the troops turned suddenly right—north—down a dirt road leading toward Hinson Mills Ford on the Rappahannock River. Soon, the crossing began four miles upstream of Pope's right flank.

First, Col. Thomas Munford's 2nd Virginia Cavalry crossed, followed by the infantry divisions of Maj. Gen. Richard Ewell, Maj. Gen. A. P. Hill, and Brig. Gen. William Taliaferro. Approximately 80 artillery pieces and a small supply train formed the column's tail.

Keeping the essence of surprise foremost in his mind, Boswell led the column not always along roads but through fields and little-known byways. His local knowledge shaved miles off the start of the long march. Through Orleans and to the outskirts of Salem where the first day's march ended after covering more than

Today, two railroads still converge at Manassas. In this modern image, you can see the enduring importance of the railroad industry in northern Virginia. (dw)

After graduating from VMI in 1852, Thomas Munford found himself in the life of a planter and railroader when the war broke out. He fought at First Manassas and, as colonel of the 2nd Virginia, led a brigade of cavalry attached to Ewell's division in the 1862 Valley campaign. (phofcw)

Major General Richard Ewell spent most of his pre-war army career in the Southwest. A West Point graduate, Ewell won a brevet for gallantry in the Mexican-American War. Ewell saw good service at First Manassas and in Jackson's Valley campaign in the spring of 1862. (na)

25 miles, Fauquier County's citizens turned out to cheer and offer food to the weary foot soldiers. Most of the march was conducted in secret, save for one spot along the road outside of Salem.

There, to view his troops, Jackson surmounted a large rock. "His sun-burned cap was lifted from his brow, and he was gazing toward the west, where the splendid August sun was about to kiss the distant crest of the Blue Ridge," recalled one of Jackson's earliest biographers. His "blue eyes, beaming with martial pride," looked upon his troops. Biographer Robert Dabney wrote what happened next:

His men burst forth into their accustomed cheers, forgetting all their fatigue at his inspiring presence; but, deprecating the tribute by a gesture, he sent an officer to request that there should be no cheering, inasmuch as it might betray their presence to the enemy. They at once repressed their applause, and passed the word down the column to their comrades: "No cheering, boys; the General requests it." But as they passed him, their eyes and gestures, eloquent with suppressed affection, silently declared what their lips were forbidden to utter. Jackson turned to his Staff, his face beaming with delight, and said: "Who could not conquer, with such troops as these?"

Jackson's march toward Salem carried his men 12 miles north of Waterloo Bridge, nearly behind Pope's army.

Without knowing it, Pope's advantage of time began to slip from his grasp. Lee was taking the initiative away from Pope, to force his army away from the Rappahannock River. But this was precisely where orders from General-in-Chief Halleck told Pope to stay and unite with the Army of the Potomac. Confusion gripped the Federal high command, with neither Pope, McClellan, nor Halleck operating on the same page. The unification of the two armies had commenced already, but it would take time for them to coalesce into one force.

Renewed cannon fire along the Rappahannock told Pope that Lee's army was still south of it. Reports reached him of a large enemy column moving north— Jackson's column—but Pope and his subordinates reached the conclusion that the enemy was not heading for his rear but instead for the Shenandoah Valley. Pope envisioned a thrust into this column's rear, though it never came to fruition.

Rather than placing troops in the direction of the column moving beyond his right, Pope instead lengthened his river line in the opposite direction where he expected the Army of the Potomac would be arriving. Bungled orders, worsened by the fluid situation present in any campaign where two opposing armies were in contact, merited no response from Pope to Jackson's column. The Army of Virginia's cavalry was in rough shape and "almost completely disorganized," Brig. Gen. John Buford said.

Pope sought to sort out affairs on his army's front. For the next morning, he ordered McDowell to perform a reconnaissance in force on the south bank of the Rappahannock River to learn what strength the Confederates maintained there.

When the sun rose on August 26, Jackson's men awoke less sure of their destination than Pope, who repeated his belief to Halleck that the column was moving toward the Shenandoah Valley. Despite the hard march of the previous day and the limited rations Jackson's men carried with them, they dutifully formed their ranks and followed directions.

At Salem, Jackson's column turned east, now pointed like a dagger straight at Pope's supply line. Looming in the distance stood the last natural obstacle Jackson's men had to navigate that the enemy might use to dispute the march: the Bull Run Mountains. Specifically, the Confederate troops marched directly for Thoroughfare Gap, a narrow pass carved through the mountains over the past centuries by Broad Run. The gap was barely wide enough to fit the stream, a road, the Manassas Gap Railroad, and a mill complex. The van of Jackson's command reached the gap and breathed a sigh of relief when no Federal troops opposed their passage. Jackson's men could now descend freely into Pope's rear.

Still grasping for information, General McDowell marched to the Rappahannock River to learn of the Confederate strength there. Longstreet's batteries positioned on high ground south of the river told McDowell the enemy was still present and in strength. Reports from elsewhere in the army filtered into Pope's headquarters that painted a clearer picture of where the wayward Confederate column was heading. One of these reports told Pope of enemy troops passing through Thoroughfare Gap, yet Pope did not worry about his supply line.

Jackson soon made him worry.

Brigadier General William Taliaferro graduated from the College of William and Mary in 1841. He received a captain's commission in the United States Army in 1847, fighting in the Mexican-American War. His association with the Virginia militia in the late 1850s, as well as the early days of the Civil War, assisted with his rise through the Confederate army until his wounding. (loc)

Like several other officers in both armies, including Pope, Brig. Gen. John Buford hailed from Kentucky. After his graduation from West Point, he put his schooling to practice seeing frontier service in Texas, New Mexico, Kansas, and elsewhere. It was Pope who got Buford promoted to brigadier general and command of the reserve cavalry brigade in Pope's new army. (loc)

Located just west of the town of Haymarket, Thoroughfare Gap was an important passageway through the Bull Run Mountains for Lee's army in August 1862. The narrow gap not only had an important road connecting towns east and west of the mountains, but also the Manassas Gap Railroad. (b&l)

With Pope stalled on the river's north bank, Lee and Longstreet decided it was time to reunite the Army of Northern Virginia. Longstreet's half of the army began marching on the afternoon of August 26 to join Jackson after he severed the Orange and Alexandria Railroad. His column, preceded by Stuart and the Confederate cavalry, followed directly in the footsteps of Jackson's men.

While events transpired along the Rappahannock River, at 4 p.m. Jackson's troops entered Gainesville, 10 miles from the Federal supply depot at Manassas Junction. Before the march began, Jackson asked Boswell to find "the most direct and covered route to Manassas." Manassas Junction, Jackson's goal, was a large Federal supply hub on the Orange and Alexandria Railroad (O&A) and a piece of northern Virginia with which Jackson was familiar from time spent there in 1861. Jackson knew the extent of the defenses built there by the Confederate army the previous year and had to assume the Federals had only strengthened them. Taking Manassas Junction might not be easy.

From Gainesville, Jackson set his sights on the next station down the line, Bristoe Station, five miles southwest of Manassas Junction. Jackson decided to cut Pope's supply line there. Before he moved, help arrived in the form of Stuart and two brigades of cavalry. Then, Jackson's march resumed once more in the direction of Bristoe Station.

Bristoe Station and the O&A Railroad had been crowded with troops in August. However, most of those troops were only passing through from the wharves of Alexandria on their way to link with the Army of Virginia farther south. Troops from Maj.

Gen. Samuel Heintzelman's III Corps, Army of the Potomac, had recently passed through Bristoe Station. They continued onto Warrenton Junction and detrained there.

Shortly after 6 p.m., as Jackson's men neared the railroad hamlet, approximately 100 Federals under Capt. John Conser defended the rail line. Colonel Thomas Munford's 2nd Virginia Cavalry learned of the weakness from locals and, under Jackson's orders, charged the station. The garrison put up a fight, but many of the surprised bluecoats scattered once Confederate infantry arrived. Without much loss, Jackson's column severed the O&A, Pope's link to reinforcements and to Washington.

No sooner had the Confederates secured the station than they heard the shrill whistle of a train approaching from the south, signaling the trains returning to Alexandria for the night. Hurriedly, Munford's horsemen and Col. Henry Forno's Louisiana infantry piled obstructions on the tracks and tried to rip them up.

A renowned Civil War historian wrote of Maj. Gen. Heintzelman, "He somehow just missed being an effective corps commander." West Point graduated, frontier and garrison service marked his early military career before the Mexican-American War. Before Second Manassas, he commanded troops at First Manassas, Yorktown, Seven Pines, and the Seven Days. (loc)

The whir of bullets greeted the crew of the "Secretary" as it neared the station. The locomotive's engineer threw his train into high speed and broke through the impromptu barrier, making it safely, though bullet-punctured, to Manassas Junction.

Confederate disappointment did not linger for long; the whistle of another approaching train burst upon their ears. Jackson's men feverishly worked to make a large section of the track impassable. The engineer of the "President" received the same greeting as the previous engineer and throttled his locomotive into high speed. Once it hit the trap laid out for it, the train tumbled off the tracks, though some of the rear cars remained upright on the rails.

Gleeful at their capture, the eyes of Jackson's men grew wider when they heard a third whistle. By now, darkness had set in. One of the quick-thinking Confederates jumped to the rear car still on the tracks and extinguished the red lights on the back of the train. Another man familiar with trains blew a signal from the "President's" cab indicating the track ahead was clear.

Lured in by Confederate trickery, the "Redbird" approached at its normal speed until the locomotive "ploughed under" the "President's" rear cars, "setting them crossways on its back and on the back of the tender. The impetus having been communicated to

Manassas Junction was a vital rail hub in northern Virginia before the war, both for commerce and transportation. It played a pivotal role during both the First and Second Manassas campaigns. (phofcw)

Twenty-two years of age when the war began, Samuel Craig worked as a printer's apprentice before attending Jefferson College in Canonsburg, Pennsylvania. He left his schooling before graduation to volunteer for service in the Federal army. (wphm)

the cars, they telescoped each other or got each other crossways on the track," one Confederate eyewitness remembered. "Many cars were forced out upon the pile over the locomotive, and the general effect was very destructive."

The wreckage of two locomotives and 24 rail cars littered the tracks and the embankment at Bristoe Station. A fourth engine approached but smartly backed off when its engineer sensed danger ahead. Jackson and his men could not have been happier with the prey they'd caught.

As Jackson surveyed the wreckage, word reached him of "stores of great value" at Manassas Junction. Desiring to keep the initiative, he ordered Brig. Gen. Isaac Trimble to take the rail junction. Trimble selected the 21st Georgia and 21st North Carolina to accomplish the nighttime mission. Stuart's cavalry soon joined them.

Manassas Junction's garrison, led by Capt. Samuel Craig, belied the sense of security Pope felt for his communication line. Craig had 115 infantrymen, 8 cannon, and the green 12th Pennsylvania Cavalry to protect the depot. They were on high alert thanks to the "Secretary's" crew that escaped the Confederate gauntlet five miles down the tracks. Craig increased his strength in the fortifications and waited.

Stuart's cavalry struck first but, in the darkness, quickly pulled back to preserve as much surprise as possible. The plan worked. Within a half-mile of the junction, Trimble arrayed his two regiments on either side of the tracks. Covered by night, they charged the Federal defenses. In five minutes, Craig's garrison scattered. At the cost of 2 men killed and 2 wounded, Trimble and Stuart captured 6 guns, approximately 300 Federals, and secured the supplies stored at Manassas Junction.

In 36 hours, Jackson's 24,000 men had marched about fifty miles, cut Pope's supply line in two places, and firmly stood in Pope's rear between him and Washington. Jackson hardly could have asked for more from his foot cavalry.

Brigadier General Isaac Trimble, despite being born in Culpeper County, Virginia, in 1802, later became a self-identified Marylander during the remainder of the antebellum era. A West Point graduate and Old Army artillery lieutenant, Trimble had long left the military in favor of the private railroad sector when the war broke out. (loc)

Largesse at the Junction

CHAPTER FIVE
NIGHT, AUGUST 26– MORNING, AUGUST 28, 1862

Optimism shone on the faces of everyone at John Pope's headquarters on August 26. Pope and his staffers believed the Confederates reportedly marching around his flank had "probably gone into the Valley." The Army of the Potomac's elements were starting to join the Army of Virginia, giving "confidence to all. The opening of the battle will no longer be a painful sound," David Hunter Strother wrote in his diary. Thus far, Pope had blunted Lee.

The passing of the "Secretary" through Bristoe Station to Manassas Junction on the night of August 26 was a blessing to Pope. The message of Confederates at Bristoe Station brought by the train's engineer spread quickly down the telegraph lines—before Jackson's men cut them—to Pope's headquarters. Within 20 minutes, at 8:20 p.m., Pope ordered the recently arrived Samuel Heintzelman to send a regiment along the tracks and determine what happened.

While Pope waited for this reconnaissance to complete its mission, word from various sources flooded into his headquarters indicating the possibility of a large force along the railroad in his rear, rather than a mere cavalry raid. Pope began to weigh the prospect that Lee's entire army was moving around his right flank. But before he could react to the potential threat, he needed firsthand information of what was happening near Manassas Junction.

That task fell to Capt. Harmon Bliss's 300 men of the 72nd New York Infantry. Bliss's orders were

The men of the Excelsior Brigade exchanged volleys with Forno's Louisianans at close range during the battle of Kettle Run. (kp)

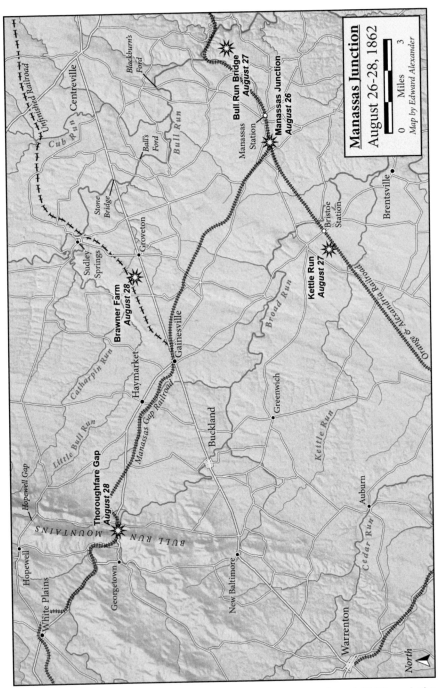

MANASSAS JUNCTION—"Stonewall" Jackson's march around Pope on August 25-26 sparked a series of fights around Manassas Junction as Pope sought to bring Jackson to a decisive battle. These smaller fights allowed Jackson to evade Pope's converging columns and draw Pope into battle on the old Bull Run battlefield.

LEFT: David Hunter Strother's family lineage included the prestigious title as one of the First Families of Virginia. He did not join the war effort until March 1862, but just six months later was promoted and served as the topographer on Pope's staff. (na)

RIGHT: At the age of 30, Harmon Bliss was older than the average Civil War soldier. Captain of Co. G, 72nd New York Infantry, he later died of wounds sustained at the battle of Chancellorsville in May 1863. (nysmm)

to "proceed at once with my command to Manassas, to ascertain what occurred, rejoin the telegraph wires, and protect the railroad there till further orders." Bliss cautiously approached within a mile of Bristoe Station with skirmishers out front. Finding the telegraph wires cut and a burning train in the distance, Bliss deployed his entire regiment in the predawn darkness. He reported, "the reflection from the burning cars enabled me from my position to see all [the enemy's] movements," and this "satisfied me that they were in force."

Bliss withdrew from Bristoe Station to the Kettle Run bridge. With the aid of a telegrapher that accompanied his regiment, Bliss wrote to Pope's headquarters that he found the enemy at Bristoe Station "in very heavy force."

News such as this might have undone some generals, but John Pope remained optimistic. As he saw it, Lee's army was strung out, stretching from the railroad to beyond the Bull Run Mountains. "The movement of Jackson presented the only opportunity which had offered to gain any success over the superior forces of the enemy," he wrote years later. That morning, Pope told McDowell of the enemy's interruption of the railroad, which "will require a strong force to repair it and keep it open." He continued, "It therefore appears to me that we had best move with our whole force to occupy Gainesville, so as to secure our communication with Alexandria." Pope moved quickly to seize the opportunity in front of him.

The commanding general ordered his army to turn away from the Rappahannock River and advance in three columns to hit Jackson's isolated portion of the Army of Northern Virginia. On the left, Maj. Gen. Irvin McDowell led 25,000 men toward Gainesville. Major General Jesse Reno's IX

Jesse Reno graduated with a who's who class of future Civil War generals at West Point in 1846, including Gens. McClellan, Jackson, and Pickett. His prewar military service was extensive and varied and by the fall of 1861 he had been promoted to brigadier general of volunteers and given a brigade in Ambrose Burnside's command. (loc)

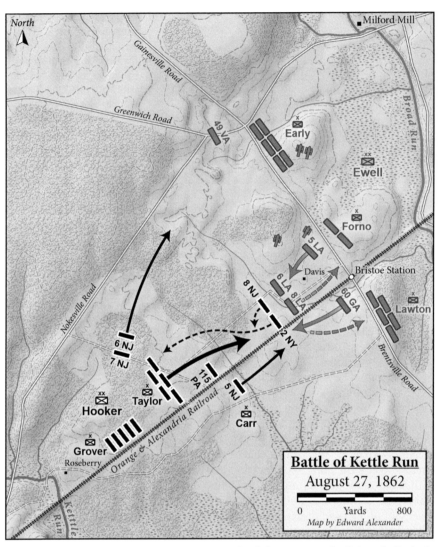

BATTLE OF KETTLE RUN—Maj. Gen. Richard Ewell's Confederates staved off Joseph Hooker's advancing Federals for a couple of hours at the battle of Kettle Run before withdrawing toward Manassas Junction. This fight made Pope believe that he could defeat Jackson singularly before the Confederate army reunited.

Corps division, supplemented by Kearny's division of Heintzelman's corps (approximately 15,000 men), formed the center column; the town of Greenwich was their destination. Heintzelman's other division under Joseph Hooker would retrace its steps along the railroad toward Alexandria to open the rail line. Fitz John Porter's V Corps formed the army's reserve while Nathaniel Banks's men guarded the army's rear. Pope expected to engage Jackson near Gainesville. Pope's

65,000 men marched to ensnare Jackson and achieve a victory over a man who only taught defeat to many of these Federal soldiers.

Some good luck smiled on the Federals that morning. While Pope advanced against Jackson from the south and west, Col. Herman Haupt and Henry Halleck also planned a response to the Confederate incursion on the O&A. Haupt formulated a plan to send a train accompanied by 4,000 men from Alexandria to repair and open the railroad. Halleck also ordered Maj. Gen. William Franklin's VI Corps to march to Gainesville. As the sun rose on August 27, 80,000 Federals were converging on the area between Gainesville and Manassas Junction.

Jackson did not know of this large Union response, but he did know he had to move quickly in order to reinforce Trimble's small command and secure the stores at Manassas Junction. A single night march had been enough, so once the sun rose on August 27, Jackson ordered Hill's and Taliaferro's divisions to the junction.

The Confederates found on the march indications of what was to come: camp debris, food, and supplies littered the landscape along the railroad left behind during the hasty Federal retreat. Once they reached the junction and the dozens of warehouses containing the supplies, their eyes widened. An artillerist remembered that the depot contained "an amount and variety of property such as I had never conceived of (I speak soberly)."

No sooner had Jackson's men dropped their rifles to pick up the supplies than the distant boom of two cannons reminded them they were still at war. Jackson

Major General Fitz John Porter, a graduate of West Point, won brevets for distinguished service during the Mexican-American War. He later taught at the academy and served in the Utah expedition before the war. At its outset he was commissioned colonel of the 15th Regular Infantry. One of Lincoln's secretaries later wrote that he was "ruined by his devotion to McClellan." (loc)

Civil War sketch artist Edwin Forbes depicted this scene of the Army of the Potomac retreating across the bridge at Kettle Run in October 1863. That bridge, depicted in the rear of the sketch, witnessed a similar scene in August 1862 by Pope's troops. (loc)

August 27, 1862, witnessed a lot of marching by the Army of Virginia. This woodcut drawing, inspired by a wartime sketch, depicts the rear of just one of many of Pope's columns on the march that day. (b&l)

ordered his men into the fortifications surrounding the junction to meet this threat.

In the distance, the hustling Confederates saw a blue battle line 600 men strong. It was Col. Gustav Waagner's 2nd New York Heavy Artillery, which had received orders the previous day to march from the forts surrounding Washington to Manassas Junction to reinforce the garrison there. After the green regiment crossed Bull Run, the Czech colonel found the remnants of Craig's force, who were anxious to retake their lost guns. Craig's artillerists opened fire (these were the two shots Jackson's men heard) and then Waagner cautiously ordered his regiment forward, supposing "that the enemy were in greater force than what was at first reported."

Waagner's men encountered some Confederate cavalry initially but soon saw the arrival of enemy infantry. Recognizing his disadvantage, Waagner wisely ordered a retreat. The brief action cost his regiment 7 men wounded and 37 captured or missing.

No sooner had Jackson's men repulsed Waagner's limited advance from the north than they saw another body of troops advancing from the east. These troops were from New Jersey, led by Brig. Gen. George Taylor. They were the force Haupt had sent the previous evening to open the O&A Railroad.

Taylor's men jumped from the train cars east of Bull Run Bridge, the span that carried the railroad across Bull Run. Leaving one regiment behind to

guard the bridge, the others dumped their unnecessary gear, formed a battle line, and advanced. Taylor was not aware of the large enemy force in front of him.

By now, Jackson's line was in a concave shape utilizing the fortifications and terrain to his men's advantage. Some 9,000 infantry and 28 guns filled the line. Anxious gunners opened fire on Taylor's New Jerseyans as they advanced; others waited until the Federals were closer. Once within Jackson's concave position, the Confederates pulled lanyards and squeezed triggers, sending a wave of iron and lead at the enemy.

Frantically, Taylor ordered his men to fix bayonets and charge against the enemy. The Confederate fire was too much, however. After a brief stand, Taylor's soldiers fell back to the bridge, pursued by enemy cavalry and infantry the whole way. Order disintegrated when the Federals reached a steep hill overlooking the span. The Confederates fired on them, and panic ensued. Taylor yelled for his officers "to prevent another Bull Run" before enemy fire mortally wounded him.

Two supporting Ohio regiments stopped the Confederates from crossing Bull Run, but the damage had already been done. Besides Taylor, of

Federal soldiers fought in this open field against Ewell's Confederates on the hot afternoon of August 27. The Confederate line stood approximately where the treeline is today. (kp)

A native of New Jersey, Brig. Gen. George Taylor had varied army and navy service before the Civil War, including service in the Mexican-American War. Taylor died of his wounds from Bull Run Bridge on September 1, 1862, in Alexandria. (loc)

the 1,200 men of the brigade, 339 of them (28%) became casualties.

Word of the disaster that befell Taylor's command reached Maj. Gen. George B. McClellan when he disembarked in Alexandria. The Federal defeat at Bull Run Bridge was the manifestation of McClellan's greatest worry: sending unsupported driblets of troops forward to find Pope and having them be pounced on by an enemy whose whereabouts were uncertain. Thus, for two days, no more soldiers of the Army of the Potomac would move toward Pope's aid.

The dual victories hyped Jackson's men to reward themselves with the spoils of their capture at Manassas Junction. Soldiers helped themselves to stores and food they would never be given in the field. Open railcars and warehouses revealed "potted ham, lobster, tongue, candy, cakes, nuts, oranges, lemons, pickles, catsup, mustard, etc. It makes an old soldier's mouth water now, to think of the good things captured there," recalled veteran John Worsham. Some Confederates also helped themselves to new arms and ammunition. Back down the line at Bristoe Station, the thunder of battle echoed in the distance, but the men of Hill's and Taliaferro's divisions paid little attention to it. They had done their share of fighting for the day.

Major General Richard Ewell's division missed out on the abundance of Manassas Junction's depots. Instead, when Jackson marched away from Bristoe Station on the morning of August 27, he ordered Ewell's brigades to remain and watch for a Federal advance from Warrenton Junction.

Bliss's morning reconnaissance showed Ewell that something would be heading in his direction. He laid out his division to meet any threat. Ewell, who grew up not far from Bristoe Station, tasked Henry Forno's Louisiana brigade with anchoring the defense. Two of Forno's regiments advanced to Kettle Run armed with orders to fall back on Bristoe Station should a large enemy force appear. Along the Brentsville Road, Ewell's two other brigades and the rest of Forno's took a position backed by 16 artillery pieces.

Joe Hooker's column had spent the morning advancing along the tracks of the railroad and sweating under the boiling sun, which pushed the temperature to 90 degrees by 2 p.m., the approximate time Hooker's van reached Kettle Run. Colonel Joseph Carr's brigade pushed Forno's 6th and 8th Louisiana back, but not before they burned the bridge over

LEFT: Joseph Hooker had a steady rise in the Old Army before the Civil War, with several brevets as a result of service in the Mexican-American War. Despite this, he resigned in the 1850s, and after five years away from the army tried unsuccessfully to secure an appointment back in as a colonel. Only the outbreak of the war saw Hooker back in command of men. (loc)

RIGHT: Colonel Joseph Carr was a tobacconist before the war, although he did have some military experience as a colonel of militia. Mustered in as colonel of the 2nd New York Infantry, he saw service at one of the earliest battles of the war, Big Bethel. (loc)

the stream. Their withdrawal did not stop until they reached a position within 300 yards of Bristoe Station.

Carr's brigade pursued the Louisianans. When they approached within less than 100 yards of Forno's two regiments, Confederate rifle and artillery fire cut up Carr's two lead regiments. "We could see the shot and shell plough through their crowded ranks and make long lanes, and we shouted for joy," an enthusiastic Confederate artillerist remembered. Hooker sought a way around the Confederate right and personally took two New Jersey regiments with him to discover the enemy's flank. The final two regiments in Carr's brigade advanced astride the railroad, but confusion and a mistaken case of friendly fire halted their progress.

Colonel Nelson Taylor led the Excelsior Brigade, also from Hooker's division, behind Carr's men. Seeing his predecessors pinned down from the enemy fire, Taylor deployed his brigade in two lines—three regiments in front and two in the rear. They advanced into the open field fronting Forno's line and added their lead to the conflict.

Forno brought another of his regiments forward into the fight, as did Brig. Gen. Alexander Lawton, whose Georgia brigade was east of the railroad. Lawton ordered the 60th Georgia forward, which obtained a position from which it could fire down the length of Taylor's line. Taylor dispatched his two rear regiments to form at right angles to his front line to confront the Georgians. Carr's other regiments along the railroad sorted themselves out and moved toward the Georgians as well, while Hooker engaged Ewell's right.

The pressure was too much for the 60th Georgia; they had to fall back. Taylor's New Yorkers sprang to their feet and surged toward the railroad. "I never have seen a handsomer sight," a New Jerseyan said of Taylor's men seizing the railroad. "[O]ne of Sickels [sic] regiments got their color planted on the track and soon Johnny rebel was skeddadling across the hill."

Ewell's line was feeling the pressure, and the general himself was sweating what his superior was thinking. Jackson had left Ewell at Bristoe Station without explicit orders. As the fight began, Ewell sent a courier back to Jackson requesting clarification. About this time, Jackson's response arrived, which told Ewell to not "allow himself to become entangled" with the enemy. This was enough for Ewell, who ordered his men to fall back behind Broad Run in the direction of Manassas Junction.

Hooker's division tried to hamper Ewell's withdrawal, but the Confederate general and his men executed it masterfully. By 6 p.m., three and a half hours after it began, the fighting at Kettle Run and Bristoe Station was over. Ewell bought Jackson's two other divisions time at the cost of 176 casualties. The Federals sustained 413 losses.

John Pope reached Bristoe Station in time to see the enemy's backs and his own army's success. Pope conferred with Hooker, whose men were low on ammunition, and Confederate prisoners, who told him that Jackson and 25,000 men were in front of him at Manassas Junction.

Pope's blood was up. His plan had so far paid off. He ordered Fitz John Porter's V Corps to join him at Bristoe Station by the next morning. "I believed then," Pope said later, "that we were sufficiently in advance of Longstreet . . . that by using our whole force vigorously we should be able to crush Jackson completely before Longstreet could have reached the scene of action." That night, Pope ordered McDowell's and Reno's columns to Manassas Junction. He told the former, "If you will march promptly and rapidly at the earliest dawn of day upon Manassas Junction we shall bag the whole crowd."

The commanding general awoke the next morning, expecting to hear battle and Jackson's demise coming from the direction of Manassas Junction. Instead, he heard nothing. A bungled march brought the first Federals to the junction at noon on August 28, and all they found was charred railcars, burnt out warehouses, whatever items Confederate soldiers could not stuff in their belongings, and a few enemy stragglers. These loose-lipped men informed Pope that he was not far behind Jackson's column, only an hour or so, and that it had gone toward Centreville.

Pope sensed how close he was to defeating Jackson. At 2 p.m., he altered his plans, ordering McDowell to pursue Jackson toward Centreville. A major clash between the two forces seemed imminent.

The Road to Brawner Farm

CHAPTER SIX

NIGHT, AUGUST 27–
5 P.M., AUGUST 28, 1862

Irvin McDowell was a troubled general on the night of August 27. All day, as his column marched toward Gainesville, Brig. Gen. John Buford's cavalry apprised McDowell of Longstreet's whereabouts. This second enemy column would pass through Thoroughfare Gap the next day. McDowell pondered what he should do about this from a piano bench in a small house near Buckland. Franz Sigel listened to McDowell's thoughts but left the final decision up to him.

Finally, McDowell hatched a plan. In the morning, Sigel's corps along with one of McDowell's divisions would go to Haymarket, four miles east of Thoroughfare Gap, to monitor and, if necessary, stop Longstreet's march. McDowell's other two divisions were to continue their trek to Gainesville and ultimately to Manassas Junction. His decision was final.

Then, Pope's orders of 9 p.m. that night, written from Bristoe Station, called on McDowell to move quickly toward Manassas Junction the next morning and eliminate Jackson's wing of the Army of Northern Virginia. If Pope's orders were carried out according to his thoughts, a great blow might be struck to Lee's army.

To comply with the commanding general's orders, McDowell scrapped his two-pronged plan and ordered Sigel's entire corps and two of his own three divisions to march on Manassas Junction in the morning. With the thought of Longstreet's column pouring through the Bull Run Mountains worryingly

The opposing lines of battle above Thoroughfare Gap fought one another across this quarry trench. One Confederate soldier wrote the lines were "close enough to have touched bayonets." (kp)

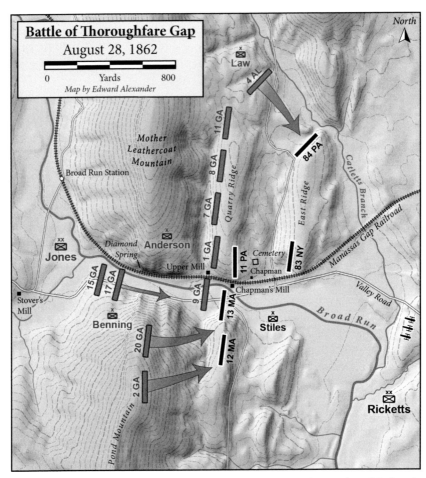

BATTLE OF THOROUGHFARE GAP—The only Federal attempt to prevent the reunion of Jackson's and Longstreet's wings of the Army of Northern Virginia was at Thoroughfare Gap in the Bull Run Mountains. Longstreet's men reached the gap before the outnumbered Federals could defend it. Following the battle, the road was open for the Confederate army to reunite.

fresh in his mind, though, McDowell's orders to his subordinates differed slightly from Pope's order to him: McDowell would not move his entire two corps force towards Jackson. Instead, he decided to leave behind one division of 5,000 men, under Brig. Gen. James Ricketts at Gainesville, to monitor Thoroughfare Gap and oppose enemy passage through it.

Pope's advance on Manassas Junction got off to a late start, and his anticipated clash with Jackson did not occur. Meanwhile, fourteen miles northwest of where Pope set his sights, Col. Percy Wyndham's 1st New Jersey Cavalry skirmished with the van of Longstreet's column.

Unlike Jackson's march to gain the rear of Pope's army, Longstreet, accompanied by Lee, marched his men at a more leisurely pace after they departed their positions on the south bank of the Rappahannock River on August 26 to reunite the army. It took Longstreet's men nearly 48 hours to reach Thoroughfare Gap when it had only taken Jackson's soldiers just over half that time. By the afternoon of August 28, when Longstreet's column approached the gap from the west, Lee ordered his subordinate to occupy the gap, bivouac the rest of his command, and rest for tomorrow, when Lee would reunite the two columns of his army.

Colonel Wyndham and the men of the 1st New Jersey Cavalry had worked fiercely to stall an enemy march through the pass, but chopping down trees and laying them across the road could only do so much. He notified his commander that he required assistance.

James Ricketts's division had not yet reached Gainesville when he received Wyndham's request. He quickly ordered his column off the Warrenton Pike to cut cross country in the direction of the gap. The day's heat and the difficult nature of the off-road march slowed the column so that it did not reach Haymarket until 2 p.m., the same time Pope was ordering his army to move toward Centreville to confront Jackson. (This would soon change for McDowell once Pope, altering his plans again, ordered McDowell to stop Longstreet.) For the moment, though, Ricketts's division would try to oppose Longstreet by itself.

As Ricketts's tired men moved west from Haymarket, Wyndham's troopers spread the ominous news that the Confederates already held the gap. Colonel John Stiles's brigade, which would experience combat for the first time this day, led the Federal column toward the gap to drive the enemy out of it.

Stiles's lead regiment, the 11th Pennsylvania, ran into the van of Col. George T. Anderson's brigade— the 9th Georgia—a quarter mile east of the gap. The Georgians staged a fighting withdrawal to buy time for the rest of Anderson's brigade to arrive.

Thoroughfare Gap was a flat gap notched between Mother Leathercoat Mountain to the north and Pond Mountain to the south. John Chapman's seven story stone mill stood between the Manassas Gap Railroad north of it and Broad Run and the Valley Road to the south.

A native of New York City, Brig. Gen. James Ricketts graduated from West Point in 1839. A rather unremarkable career in the Old Army followed. Wounded four times and captured at First Manassas, he was not exchanged until January 1862. (loc)

Born at sea, Col. Percy Wyndham served with various countries' militaries before coming to the U.S. and serving in the Union army, although much of his history is dubious. Captured in June 1862, he had only been recently exchanged before the Second Manassas campaign. (loc)

Nestled in Thoroughfare Gap, and on the border between Prince William and Fauquier Counties in Virginia, the Beverley Chapman mill was constructed in 1742 by father and son Jonathan and Nathaniel Chapman. The prosperity of the mill continued unabated with numerous expansions, and, on the cusp of the Civil War, stood at seven stories. In 1998 the mill was largely destroyed by fire lit by an arsonist. The stabilized remnants serve as a reminder of the history the mill and its owners witnessed over the centuries. (loc)

Colonel Henry Benning had an impressive law career during the antebellum years, including time as an associate justice of the Georgia Supreme Court. His notoriety in the state sent him to numerous secession conventions, including as a delegate to Virginia's. His military career in the Confederacy began as colonel of the 17th Georgia Infantry. (loc)

Stiles deployed the rest of his brigade. Backed up by Ricketts's artillery, they advanced toward the gap, driving the 9th Georgia back onto the rest of Anderson's brigade. In the gap itself, Anderson's men began to oppose the Federal drive. Colonel Henry Benning's Georgia brigade arrived and began ascending Pond Mountain to strike Stiles's left flank. The ascent, though, was tough. Benning said, "The ground in some places was almost precipitous and everywhere was covered with stiff bushes." Nonetheless, they beat the 13th Massachusetts to the top.

Anderson extended his line north of the mill to occupy Mother Leathercoat Mountain, where they encountered the 11th Pennsylvania. This fight was close quarters and intense. At one point, the two opponents fought from opposite sides of a quarry trench, "close enough to have touched bayonets," a Confederate noted. Anderson's men began driving the Federals back. The mountainous terrain was covered with briars and underbrush, making any movement difficult, but still the Pennsylvanians managed to rally and move again to the contested quarry trench. They drove Anderson's Georgians down the western slope of the mountain. Soon, more of Anderson's men entered the fray and regained the upper hand north of the gap.

With the Confederates controlling both mountains towering over the gap, Ricketts pulled his men back to a ridge a quarter mile to the east.

Lee and Longstreet, who monitored the fight from a hill west of the mountain range, knew they had to force Ricketts back in order to facilitate the junction of the army's two wings. Orders went to Cadmus Wilcox to take his division six miles north to Hopewell Gap and descend on Ricketts's right and rear. Evander Law's brigade also scaled Mother Leathercoat Mountain to harass the Federal right. Additionally, Benning's men pressed forward against Ricketts's left. Faced with all this pressure, Ricketts had no choice but to order his division back to Gainesville.

The fight at Thoroughfare Gap cost both sides approximately 100 men combined. But the Confederate occupation of the gap gave Longstreet and Lee an open road to form a junction with Jackson's half of the army.

Colonel George T. Anderson, born in Georgia in 1824, left Emory College to fight in the Mexican-American War. Following the war, he accepted a commission into the regular army, serving just three years. He began the Civil War as colonel of the 11th Georgia Infantry. (vhs)

Meanwhile, at Manassas Junction, the sounds of battle from Thoroughfare Gap reached Pope's ears. So too did reports from Wyndham and McDowell about Longstreet's march to the gap. Pope, based on information received from Confederate stragglers at the rail junction who stated Jackson's command had marched to Centreville, changed his previous orders written that morning; now his army was to pursue Jackson in the direction of Centreville.

The news from Thoroughfare Gap, though, troubled Pope, who now realized how close Longstreet was. He told McDowell to stop his march at Gainesville to confront the second half of the Confederate army. However, over the next couple of afternoon hours, information continued to reach Pope telling of Jackson's march to Centreville, Pope's original prey. Pope could not get Jackson out of his mind. At 5 p.m., he changed plans again and ordered his army to concentrate on Centreville. McDowell turned his back on Longstreet and put his column on the Warrenton Pike heading east, to Bull Run and beyond, to bag Jackson.

Centreville was established in 1792. During 1861-1862 it became a heavily-fortified supply depot for Confederate forces and, later, Federal forces. Confederates built a spur of the O&A Railroad here, making it the first exclusively military-use railroad. Edwin Forbes created this sketch of those defenses in April 1862. (loc)

A Regular Stand-Up Fight

CHAPTER SEVEN

AUGUST 28, 1862

By 7 a.m. on the morning of Thursday, August 28, 1862, the mercury already hovered at 74 degrees in Washington, D.C. The sun had creased the horizon not more than 90 minutes earlier, yet Jackson's command was anything but idle. Over the past four days, Jackson's wing had accomplished both its strategic and tactical objectives. Strategically, Jackson had led his men into the rear of Pope's Army of Virginia. Tactically, Jackson's troops not only cut Pope's communications rearward, but also crippled a major supply depot and transportation network. Although these setbacks could be repaired in several days, they could not have occurred at a worse time.

Despite these successes, Stonewall refused to sit on his laurels at Manassas Junction. Orders had filtered down through Jackson's command not twelve hours earlier. Once again, his foot cavalry was on the march.

Their next destination was to the west, a position that not only placed them closer to Longstreet's wing and the reunification of the army, but also where he could finally bring Pope to battle once more. Thus, Jackson chose a location north of the Warrenton Turnpike at Groveton, a line that ran from Groveton proper to Sudley Springs. Once there and his three divisions reunited, Jackson's line quickly demonstrated its strength and sound tactical planning.

The strong defensive position included a significant ridgeline and use of an unfinished railroad embankment. Furthermore, the position flanked one

Looking toward the Brawner Farm, the serenity of this modern view conceals the carnage of the hard-fought engagement on August 28, 1862. (dw)

The line that Jackson chose on August 28 to place his command had numerous defensively strong attributes, including this unfinished railroad cut. (dw)

of the most important roads for troop movements and logistical support, the Warrenton Turnpike. Tactically, this line covered the road from Haymarket to Sudley Springs, a crucial "Plan B" for both Jackson and Longstreet should the latter's column be blocked on its way to connect with Jackson. Lastly, if Pope was able to land a victory blow against Jackson's column before Longstreet arrived to his relief, Jackson could retreat westward via a road from Sudley Springs, a road that led to and through Aldie Gap and into the Loudoun Valley.

*   *   *

On the late evening of August 27, as Jackson's men prepared to get on the march, John Pope laid out plans to bag Jackson at Manassas Junction. Unfortunately for Pope, Jackson's abandonment of the junction made Pope's plans obsolete. When Pope finally arrived, he came upon a scene of ruin and very few Union troops. It was here, at the junction, that Pope erroneously learned that Jackson had gone to Centreville and thus ordered his army to catch Jackson there.

Within the hour, however, Pope changed his mind. Major General Irvin McDowell, commanding the Army of Virginia's III Corps, had apprised the commanding general that General Longstreet was moving through Thoroughfare Gap. Now Pope issued orders for portions of his army to move toward Gainesville to stop Longstreet's movement, but again, within an hour, Pope vacillated on his orders. He had received fresher intelligence that indicated Jackson's army had indeed moved toward Centreville. The time neared 4 p.m. After yet another hour to consider the veracity of this intelligence, Pope now ordered his army back toward Centreville.

From the Army of the Potomac, Pope ordered Maj. Gens. Philip Kearny, Jesse Reno, and Joseph Hooker's divisions to approach Centreville from the southwest, while Maj. Gen. Irvin McDowell's corps, and specifically Brig. Gen. John F. Reynolds's division, as well as Franz Sigel's units from the Army of Virginia were ordered to move from their positions west of the junction along the Warrenton Turnpike.

At approximately 5 p.m., McDowell received the orders from Pope to move toward Centreville once again. At that time, McDowell only had one division at his immediate disposal with which to march to Centreville, that of Brig. Gen. Rufus King. This division presently rested about a mile south of the Warrenton Pike, the route which they were ordered to take, along Pageland Lane. To reach Centreville, King's division would first backtrack to the turnpike before moving eastward, ultimately passing through the village of Groveton along its way. This route would take it directly across Jackson's front, exposing its flank while in columns of four, a weak and perilous position for any infantry unit. It was one of the tactical benefits of the position Jackson had selected, and now was the time for Jackson to capitalize on it. McDowell, unaware of the peril, gave King the necessary orders to march and rode off in search of Pope.

It was the moment Jackson had waited for all day. Earlier on August 28, some of Jackson's men had captured a Union courier. From him they had learned that at least a portion of the Army of Virginia would move across their front later that day. Jackson had two false starts, however. The first troops to move across his front came around noon, but by the time the troops were ready to attack, their foe had marched far beyond their front. This story later repeated itself when an Army of Virginia wagon train moved along the Warrenton Pike. Yet again it appeared as a tiny dot on a distant horizon by the time Jackson's men were ready to attack. But Jackson was not idle between these missed opportunities. He "rode about all day in a restless way," and "mostly alone," remembered W. W. Blackford. His staff gave him a wide berth that afternoon. Blackford continued, "he was cross as a bear, and neither Generals nor staff liked to come near him if they could help it."

By the time King's division moved across Stonewall's front, however, the bear was far more relaxed. A courier had arrived with a dispatch from

West Point graduate and Mexican-American War veteran Brig. Gen. John F. Reynolds was the Commandant of Cadets and instructor of tactics at West Point when the war commenced. He was captured on June 28 and exchanged on August 8, weeks before the battle. (loc)

Hailing from a prominent American family lineage and well-educated, Brig. Gen. Rufus King resigned his commission from the U.S. Army just three years after graduating from West Point. His career for the next two decades predominantly focused on owning and editing various newspapers. Although he organized the famed Iron Brigade, his early role in the illustrious unit is often forgotten today. (loc)

General Lee informing Jackson that Longstreet's wing and Lee himself would be through Thoroughfare Gap the next morning. Blackford, who had since gone looking for some buttermilk he had heard about, returned to find Jackson after he had received the good news. He was "in the best of humor since receiving the dispatch from General Lee," Blackford recalled. He offered Jackson some of this rare treat from his canteen, and after "Old Stonewall had taken a long, deep draught, and there was not much left . . . I handed round to the other officers present."

Not long after Jackson took a moment to shake the stress of the day off with the relief of Lee's dispatch and some buttermilk, the head of King's division appeared on the Warrenton Turnpike. Jackson rode out some distance in front of his line to get a better view of the approaching Federal column. He rode back and forth, almost as if pacing while on horseback, all the while in view of King's division less than a quarter mile away. "Presently General Jackson pulled up suddenly, wheeled and galloped toward us," wrote Blackford, "and, touching his hat in military salute, said in as soft a voice as if he had been talking to a friend in ordinary conversation, 'Bring out your men, gentlemen!'"

The many officers gathered there on horseback quickly rode to their commands. The cacophony of verbal orders ringing out, accouterments and arms clinking and clanging, and the rustle of thousands of feet falling into line of battle rippled throughout the woodlot in which Jackson's men had rested and chatted throughout the day. Several pieces of Jackson's artillery moved toward the division's right flank. Once there, the guns dropped trail and opened.

While these guns were on the move, Brig. Gen. John Gibbon, commanding a brigade of Midwesterners in King's division, rode just ahead of his leading regiment. Gibbon's brigade was the second brigade in the line of march toward Centreville. Brigadier General John P. Hatch's brigade, the lead brigade, was already well ahead of Gibbon's column by this time and had "disappeared behind another piece of woods in our front," according to Gibbon. Just north of the Warrenton Turnpike, Gibbon rode to the top of what he called "a gentle rise" in order "to look around." As he scanned the landscape around him, he noticed a number of horses leaving a woodlot to his left. The horses presented their flanks to Gibbon who, as an

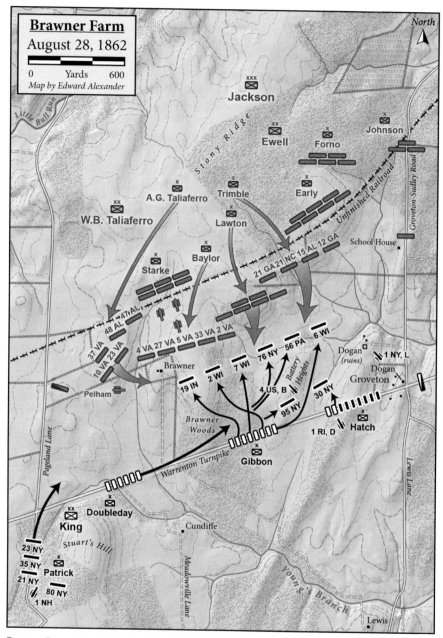

Brawner Farm
August 28, 1862

0   Yards   600
Map by Edward Alexander

North

Jackson

Ewell

Forno

Johnson

A.G. Taliaferro

Trimble

Early

W.B. Taliaferro

Lawton

School House

Baylor

Starke

21 GA 21 NC 15 AL 12 GA

48 AL 47 AL

4 VA 27 VA 5 VA 33 VA 2 VA

37 VA

76 NY 56 PA

6 WI

Dogan
(ruins)

1 NY, L

10 VA 23 VA

Brawner

19 IN 2 WI 7 WI

4 US, B

Battery Heights

Dogan

Groveton

Pelham

Brawner Woods

95 NY

30 NY

1 RI, D

Hatch

Gibbon

Warrenton Turnpike

Doubleday

King

Cundiffe

Stuart's Hill

23 NY

35 NY

Patrick

21 NY

80 NY

1 NH

Meadowville Lane

Young's Branch

Lewis

Lewis Lane

Pageland Lane

Little Bull Run

Stony Ridge

Unfinished Railroad

Groveton-Sudley Road

BRAWNER FARM—The fight at the Brawner farm was one of the most intense firefights of the entire Civil War. Jackson revealed his location to Pope during this battle, and Pope ordered his army to converge on Jackson's line the next day.

Brigadier General John Gibbon's family left Pennsylvania for North Carolina very early in his life. Thus, when he stayed in the Federal army following the secession crisis he saw three of his brothers join the Confederate army. Gibbon's role at Gettysburg often overshadows his early association with the Iron Brigade. (loc)

old artillery officer, realized that this group of horses were not enemy or friendly cavalry, but rather artillery going into battery. Gibbon immediately sent one of his staff officers to the rear of his column to bring up his own battery of artillery, 4th United States, Battery B.

It was not long before the Confederate guns opened, with one of their first rounds bursting near Gibbon. The burst of the first shells came as a shock to Gibbon's men stretched out in column along the pike. Gibbon later wrote, "Never was there a more complete surprise."

With artillery support moments away, Gibbon now turned to getting his infantry under cover and ready for possible action. He ordered his column to halt, load, and lie down in the road and along the pike in the shelter of Brawner's Woods. After observing some of Battery B's first shots, Gibbon rode off to Brawner's Woods as well, finding a vantage point where he could better assess the impact his guns made on the Confederate artillery.

Not long after he arrived at this new post, he heard more artillery fire erupt. These Confederate guns targeted the next Federal brigade in line after Gibbon's. This brigade was under the command of Brig. Gen. Abner Doubleday. The fire upon the infantry of Doubleday's brigade was just as shocking to the troops on the turnpike as was the fire that had opened on Gibbon's units.

Doubleday also ordered his men into the shelter of the trees that Brawner's Woods provided. Confederate artillery now ranged on the last of King's brigades marching along the Warrenton Turnpike, Brig. Gen. Marsena Patrick's all-New York brigade. Also surprised by the fire, the 80th New York simply fled in the face of the first several shells that landed around them. Those of the 80th that remained, as well as the

In 1860, this oak woodlot was approximately 45 acres in size. It was located on the southeast corner of the property rented by John C. Brawner, and spanned both sides of the Warrenton Pike. The woodlot, following the vicious combat of August 28, 1862, became known as Brawner's or Gibbon's Woods. (kp)

rest of Patrick's brigade, were ordered into the shelter of the woods, with some skirmishers being sent out.

The time neared 6:30 p.m. All of King's brigades were under enemy artillery fire while his artillery was either already in action or going into the fight. The infantry of his division was in perilous shape, the brigades stretched out over two miles along the turnpike, most under cover along the road or in woodlots. Even worse, division commander General King was nowhere to be found. Officers and staff later learned that just as the Confederate artillery was about to engage Gibbon's brigade, King had collapsed on the ground. Lieutenant E. K. Parker wrote in an article in 1892 that "at first [I] thought that he had been struck by a shell, or a bullet, but soon saw that he was in a severe epileptic fit." Parker recognized the signs of a seizure as he'd had a childhood friend who had suffered from them quite frequently. King was unable to prosecute the battle that had just begun.

Brigadier General Abner Doubleday came from a prominent American family and was present inside Fort Sumter when it was fired upon in April 1861. (loc)

Meanwhile, back along the Warrenton Pike, generals Gibbon and Doubleday met to discuss what to do next. Although Doubleday ranked Gibbon, he was new to the division and felt he needed King's agreement before making any orders. But King was incapacitated. Both Gibbon and Doubleday did agree, however, that the Confederate artillery fire needed to be silenced. Gibbon took that as Doubleday's blessing to order an attack against the artillery. He ordered the veteran 2nd Wisconsin into the fight.

When the orders to advance reached the men of the regiment, Sheldon Judson wrote that "an usual sensation of impending ill pervaded my mind." After advancing nearly a quarter mile forward from the pike, the regiment came within musket range. During their advance they had driven in the Confederate skirmishers, and now a "very heavy musketry fire was opened" on the Wisconsin men. Colonel Edgar O'Connor, commander of the 2nd, had instructions to fire a volley at this position and then double-quick to capture the Confederate artillery before they could recover. The erratic fire from the 2nd during their advance, and the Confederate skirmishers returning to the main line, notified the artillerists that it was time to pull out. Although the guns were now silenced, they were not captured.

The Stonewall Brigade, under the command of Col. William S. H. Baylor, concealed on the wooded ridgeline, advanced toward the lone Federal regiment.

With an erratic professional career following his flight from home early in life and before admission to West Point, Marsena Patrick graduated near the bottom of his class. His military service before he resigned in 1850 was unremarkable. It was George McClellan who got him a brigadier's commission and a brigade in Rufus King's division. (na)

Lieutenant Ezra K. Parker
served in both Battery D and
E, First Rhode Island Light
Artillery during the war. He
was originally from Coventry,
Rhode Island. Parker wrote
a stirring account of his
battery's actions during the
Overland campaign in 1864.
(pn)

Once in line of battle, they "all advanced in as perfect order as if they had been on parade . . . the light of the setting sun and their red battle flags dancing gayly in the breeze," remembered Blackford. One Confederate who watched their deployment recalled, "It made one's blood tingle with pride to see these troops going into action" and that they were going into the fight "with the confidence of veterans who had won every battle they ever fought." Although some of Gibbon's men opened fire as the Confederate brigade reached 150 yards from their position, most stood firm, awaiting the gap to close even further before loosing a round. The randomness of fire coming from the 2nd's line during the Confederate advance did not slow down Baylor's attack. The all-Virginia brigade pushed on until they reached a fence line just 80 yards from the Federal battle line.

Now the Virginians opened fully on the 450 muskets of the 2nd Wisconsin. In the 33rd Virginia, a regiment in the Stonewall Brigade, Pvt. John O. Casler recalled that they were fighting from behind an old fence, lying down to load and fire. The 2nd Wisconsin's return fire was so hot that "[E]very one who would raise up was shot."

Gibbon, "finding that the regiment had become badly involved," then "ordered the rest of the brigade rapidly up to its support." These new regiments added more than 1,000 more men, extending the line of battle to the left and right of the 2nd. For the next thirty minutes, the 800 men of Baylor's brigade blazed away at the lengthening Federal line. The fighting along the Stonewall Brigade's front was extremely costly. Realizing the intensity of the fire signaled added weight to the enemy line, Jackson sent in the all-Georgia brigade under the command of Brig. Gen. Alexander R. Lawton to support the Stonewall Brigade's left.

Gibbon's brigade was now in serious trouble. He had committed his entire brigade, with no reserves left to come to its aid. Now arrayed against the overwhelming numbers of two Confederate brigades, Gibbon repeatedly sent requests for assistance from King at division headquarters, but King could not be located. Gibbon next sent pleas to the next two brigades in line, those of Doubleday and Patrick. Doubleday sent two of his regiments forward to assist Gibbon, and when another Federal battery came on the field and needed infantry support, Doubleday released his last regiment.

By 7:15 p.m., Jackson had sent yet another brigade against the Federal line. He wanted to keep applying pressure on the Federal right, where Gibbon's last regiment, the 6th Wisconsin, had gone into position and Doubleday's two New York regiments had come to their support on their left. These Confederate units were under the command of Brig. Gen. Isaac R. Trimble. William C. Oates of the 15th Alabama, a regiment in Trimble's brigade, remembered that as the sun set and firing grew in intensity, "everything around was lighted up by the blaze of musketry and explosion of balls like a continuous bright flash of lightning."

Despite applying an overwhelming amount of pressure through numerous regiments and sheer numbers of men, Jackson was unable to break the Federal right or center. Gibbon's and Doubleday's men refused to yield ground, even in the face of volley fire less than 80 yards distant. A stalemated battle against smaller numbers was the last thing Jackson had intended when his units went forward an hour earlier.

Jackson now shifted the fighting to the Federal left flank. There, Confederate Col. Alexander G. Taliaferro's brigade would be supported by Maj. John Pelham's horse artillery. A concerted push against the 19th Indiana by these Confederate units should have been enough to break Gibbon's flank and force the Federal line from the field, Jackson reasoned.

Darkness settled over the field of battle by the time this latest effort against the Federals was underway. Fighting swirled across John Brawner's farm. Pelham's artillery dropped their gun trails not more than 100 yards from the Hoosiers. Captain William W. Dudley of Company B wrote just weeks after the battle that they "had been firing but a few moments when a Rebel battery" appeared on their left flank. At only 50 yards apart, the Hoosiers stood like iron. "The balls fell like hail but I saw no man run. Everyone stood up and fought like men," an Indiana private wrote. But, he continued, "it was no use; they had too many men for us." General Gibbon, who had directed his brigade and the battle from their left flank, nearest the Hoosiers, ordered the regiment to withdraw.

Not long into the 8 o'clock hour, the heaviest sounds of the battle slowed significantly. Only sporadic reports were heard along the lines. Gibbon's and Doubleday's men were pulled back to the shelter

A modern view taken from Battery Heights—a post-battle, post-war name given to the area where Capt. Joseph Campbell's Battery B, 4th U.S. Artillery deployed on August 28. Capt. William Chapman's Dixie Artillery deployed here on August 30 as part of the Confederate artillery fire into the flank of the Federal attack. (dw)

of Brawner's Woods once more. "This fight was the 'baptism of fire' of my brigade," wrote Gibbon, and "for over an hour the most terrific musketry fire I have ever listened to rolled along those lines of battle. It was a regular stand up fight during which neither side yielded a foot." Although he was "exceedingly proud of the way my command had behaved in the presence of what was evidently a much superior force," Gibbon knew they had paid a heavy price for their iron mettle on the battlefield and was "saddened by my very heavy losses."

By now, Rufus King had resumed his command responsibilities, having recovered from his earlier seizure. It was 9:30 p.m., and the only remaining sounds coming from the field were the cries of the wounded and moans of the dying. Independent search parties from both sides looked in vain for their lost comrades in the darkness.

Back at Army of Virginia headquarters, Pope had monitored the engagement with much interest from a hill just east of Blackburn's Ford along the road to Centreville. From his vantage point, Pope and his staff observed the "continually rising volumes of white smoke" and "the blaze of the guns and the course of the shells over the tree-tops." Pope concluded that the fight was King meeting Jackson's wing retreating from Centreville and, promisingly, King had placed his division between Jackson and his reunification with Longstreet and Lee. As such, Pope issued new orders. King's division was to hold its position near Groveton. Ultimately those orders never reached King. Meanwhile, orders were sent to Brig. Gen. John Reynolds and Maj. Gen. Franz Sigel. Reynolds's division and Sigel's corps had arrived at and in the vicinity of Henry Hill earlier that evening. Their position was a mere mile from Jackson's line. Pope's orders to Reynolds and Sigel were to "attack the enemy vigorously at daylight the next morning." The rest of the Army of Virginia and the arriving units of the Army of the Potomac in the coming days would follow these units in their push against Jackson.

Nearing 10 p.m., most of King's division was asleep, minus those on guard and picket duty or those employed in the task of caring for the wounded and dying. With the battle over, the cost of the fight became readily apparent. Despite a front of just over a half mile in length, the numbers engaged in the small confines of the battle space produced astonishing casualties. William Blackford "rode out over the field to examine it" after the fighting trailed off. When he wrote his reminiscences of his wartime experiences years later, he could still plainly recall how "The lines [of battle] were well marked by the dark rows of bodies stretched out on the broomsedge field, lying just where they had fallen, with their heels on a well-defined line." General Gibbon, who rode over the battlefield in 1863, could still "plainly trace out the line of battle they had occupied by the half-buried bodies and the cartridge papers." One historian estimated that nearly one of every three soldiers that had participated in the fight had been shot.

After midnight, King's division stirred in to activity. King ordered his command to prepare to march to Manassas Junction. Sleeping soldiers were roused, guards and pickets slowly and quietly pulled back from their positions, and as many wounded as could be gathered to march were assisted into the column. Treating the vast number of wounded and preparing those that could fall back with the division was an enormous task. It was not until "1 o'clock in the morning [that we] left the pike and commenced the march towards Manassas Junction," Gibbon wrote.

While King's division trudged, exhausted, through the early morning hours of August 29, Confederate William Blackford rode across the Brawner farm battlefield in the early light. He saw "regular details . . . engaged in removing the wounded, many friends of the wounded and dead were wandering about the field looking up their friends, ministering to their wants, or taking last messages sent by those who were expecting to die."

Major General Richard S. Ewell was severely wounded while leading a regiment forward against John Gibbon's men. As one witness said: "[T]he knee-cap [was] split half in two, the head of the tibia knocked into several pieces & that the ball had followed the marrow of the bone for six inches breaking the bone itself into small splinters, & finally had split into two pieces on a sharp edge of bone." The bullet finally came to rest in the muscles of Ewell's calf. Ewell's leg was amputated above the knee the next day at 2:00 p.m. The loss of his leg left lasting scars on both his leg and, to many contemporaries and later historians, his command performance. The amputation took place at a home called Auburn, which was located just in front of this modern home. The house and grounds are privately owned; please do not trespass. (dw)

A Terrific and Deadly Intensity

CHAPTER EIGHT

AUGUST 29, 1862

The predawn hours of August 29 found Jackson's men still dealing with the results of the fighting just hours before at the Brawner farm. Burial details were hard at work, while wounded were still being brought in for treatment. Perhaps most jarring to Jackson and his command as the sun broke the horizon that morning was the disappearance of his foe from the previous evening. Rufus King's division, with all who were able, had marched away from the battlefield after midnight toward Centreville. Although the threat on his right was gone, it was not long before a new opponent found Jackson's position further toward his center and left.

Major General Franz Sigel, commanding the Army of Virginia's I Corps, did not allow Jackson much time for contemplation, recovery, or redeployment from the previous evening's fight. Sigel had received orders late on the 28th to "attack the enemy vigorously" on the morning of the 29th. Now, at 6:30 a.m., his artillery posted on Henry Hill and Chinn Ridge opened on Jackson's line.

"Stonewall" immediately responded to this new threat, shuffling units to various positions along the line of the unfinished railroad. Jackson's new line placed Brig. Gen. William B. Taliaferro's division, now commanded by Brig. Gen. William E. Starke, on his right. The center of Jackson's position, much more wooded than his right, consisted of two brigades of infantry from Maj. Gen. Richard S. Ewell's division.

General Hood's reconnaissance in force on the evening of August 29 pushed through the hamlet of Groveton and past the home of Lucinda Dogan and her children. They moved to this home in 1860 after their residence, "Peach Grove," had burned. (dw)

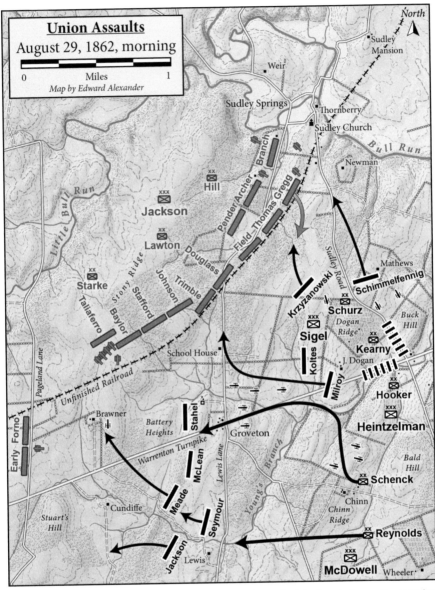

UNION ASSAULTS, AUGUST 29, 1862, MORNING—Pope's attacks against Jackson's line on the morning of August 29 were meant to fix Jackson in place while a column marching from Manassas Junction to Gainesville struck Jackson's exposed right flank. The plan fell apart quickly, and Pope's assaults throughout the day were disjointed and met with only limited successes.

Ewell's wounding the night before meant Brig. Gen. Alexander Lawton now commanded the division.

Finally, on Jackson's left flank, was Maj. Gen. A. P. Hill's division. On Hill's extreme left, and thus the extreme left of Jackson's entire position, was a brigade of South Carolinians under the command of Brig. Gen. Maxcy Gregg. They occupied a rocky knoll not far from Sudley Church. Hill, and thus Gregg, needed to ensure the crossings and fords of two waterways, Bull Run and Catharpin Run, were covered in this sector. Because Longstreet's wing was still not on the field to support Jackson, if he needed to retreat and pull his line back to the north, his troops would have to cross these runs; thus, they must be secured and not lost during any possible attack against this portion of the line.

Meanwhile, as Jackson shuttled units across his front in response to Sigel's artillery, the latter's five brigades occupied a mile-wide front and prepared to step off. Brigadier General John F. Reynolds's Pennsylvania Reserves division added three more brigades as support to Sigel's left. As the time neared 7 a.m., these infantry units advanced. Before long, they came under fire from Confederate artillery as well as Confederate skirmishers. Just an hour later, by 8 a.m., all of Sigel's and Reynolds's units were in combat against Jackson's line. The units on the left and center of this attack were content to only discover the Confederate position and determine its strength, not drive forward a victory-winning assault. But it was on the right of Sigel's attack where heavy fighting erupted almost instantly, a battle that drew in reinforcements for the remainder of the day.

A brigade commanded by Col. Wlodzimierz Krzyzanowski drove forward toward Jackson's left

Brigadier General William E. Starke was a cotton broker in Mobile and New Orleans when the war began. Following his time as aide-de-camp to Gen. R. S. Garnett in the failed West Virginia campaign, he was commissioned colonel of the 60th Virginia Infantry. Promoted to brigadier just three weeks before Second Manassas, he commanded Jackson's division in the wake of General Taliaferro's wounding. (tu)

Although services in the Sudley area can be traced to the late 18th century, it was not until between the 1820s-1840s that the first church was constructed. The First and Second battles of Manassas damaged the church beyond repair, and the church was rebuilt on the original foundation in 1873. (loc)

A prewar lawyer and Mexican-American War veteran, Brig. Gen. Maxcy Gregg was an outspoken proponent of states rights and at the outbreak of the war was commissioned as colonel of the 1st South Carolina Infantry, and by the winter of 1861 was promoted to brigadier general. (b&l)

Swept up in the revolutionary tides of Europe, Col. Wlodzimierz Krzyzanowski was forced to flee to the United States in 1846 where he took up work as a civil engineer in New York. His connections to the German community and ability to raise regiments for the Union war effort ensured a rapid rise through the ranks with Lincoln's support. (loc)

after they stepped off. Their direction of advance took them to a position inside a woodlot and the eastern edge of the unfinished railroad. There, Gregg's South Carolinians and Col. Edward L. Thomas's Georgians opposed them. The South Carolinians had not been in their position west of the cut long before their brigade commander ordered them forward, across the cut itself, and to attack the Union brigade opposite them. Shortly into their advance, the South Carolinians began trading shots with Krzyzanowski's brigade. Gregg funneled more units from his brigade into the fight. So too did his Federal foe, and by 10 a.m., after nearly two hours of fighting, the battle had drastically grown in size.

Unlike the center and left of his attacking force, Sigel was unwilling to let go of the gains that Krzyzanowski's men had made. He ordered Col. Alexander Schimmelfenning's brigade across the Sudley Road to shore up Krzyzanowski's right flank. The added reinforcements once again placed pressure on the flank and front of the South Carolinians. Gregg's men pushed forward in response, and the seesaw nature of the fighting seen since 8 a.m. continued. Eventually, Gregg ordered his brigade back to the rocky knoll where they had originally gone into position hours earlier. Federal regiments kept up their pressure as the South Carolinians pulled back. Gregg's brigade continued to warmly fire upon the advancing Federals.

At the same time Jackson's left became pressured by Sigel's morning attack, relief met Jackson on his right. Sometime around 8 o'clock, John Cussons, a courier from General Longstreet, found Jackson. When Cussons reined in his mount close enough to look at Jackson, he remembered that "he looked agitated. His face was drawn and sunburnt and his features were working." Within shouting distance now, Cussons yelled, "Longstreet's through the Gap, and I reckon at Haymarket by this time." Jackson questioned Cussons on the marching order of Longstreet's column and instantly ordered his staff officers to meet them as they arrived and show them into position.

Once Longstreet's wing finished its deployment, the Confederate line stretched for over three miles. "Old Pete's" line of battle extended Jackson's position southward over a mile alone, across the Warrenton Pike and all the way to the Manassas-Gainesville Road.

*   *   *

While Longstreet's column marched toward Jackson's relief, and fighting continued along "Stonewall's" center and left, John Pope tried to manage the growing battle from headquarters back in Centreville. Just after 10 a.m., Pope received two separate dispatches. One dispatch, from III Corps commander McDowell, conveyed his confusion and frustration that King's division was removed from his command. Now McDowell requested that his battered division be returned to him.

The second dispatch Pope received was from Maj. Gen. Fitz John Porter, commander of the V Corps of the Army of the Potomac. Porter's dispatch requested Pope to provide him with written orders and expectations for the V Corps.

Pope's response was what became known as the "Joint Order," written at 10 a.m. This order was written incredibly poorly and lacked clarity about what Pope's plans were for Porter and McDowell. All in one dispatch, Porter and McDowell were told to move "toward Gainesville," not to it; to halt once their column established communication with the rest of the army; to be in a position "from which they can reach Bull Run to-night or by morning," a retrograde movement; and gave the two commanders the leeway to depart from Pope's unclear intent "if any considerable advantages are to be gained" by doing so.

By the time Pope rode toward the field of battle after writing the Joint Order, Franz Sigel's corps was in a precarious position. The battle over the previous two hours revealed to the I Corps commander not only the true depth of Jackson's position, but also that he was sorely in need of reinforcements. Initially, Sigel responded by adding additional artillery to his line. He then sent orders to Brig. Gen. Robert Schenck, his First Division commander, to shift to his right to better support his center.

Although reinforcements began to arrive, as the ranking officer on the field Sigel had to oversee their deployment. Upon their arrival, Sigel sent Maj. Gen. Philip Kearny's division to support his wavering right flank, Maj. Gen. Joseph Hooker's division to his center, and Maj. Gen. Jesse Reno's division to various positions across his front. Over the next 90 minutes, between 10 and 11:30 a.m., Sigel's reinforcements continued to arrive. Kearny's division was supposed

Georgian Edward L. Thomas was a graduate of Emory College and veteran of the Mexican-American War, having served as a second lieutenant of Georgia mounted volunteers. He was appointed as colonel of the 35th Georgia Infantry in October 1861, a regiment he himself recruited with the blessing of Confederate President Jefferson Davis. (phofcw)

Veteran, lawyer, politician, and judge, Brig. Gen. Robert Milroy was practicing law in Rensselaer, Indiana at the beginning of the war. He saw service under McClellan in western Virginia in 1861 and then in the Shenandoah Valley campaign in the spring of 1862. (loc)

to move forward into the battle once in position, but it never did.

With the intensity of the battle growing, and Sigel's calls for reorganization of his line and reinforcements, Brig. Gen. Robert Milroy of his own volition sent two of his regiments toward the beleaguered Union right. During their movement, however, the regiments' direction unnaturally shifted, and instead of taking them further to the right to the support of Schurz's brigades, Milroy's regiments marched directly toward the Confederate center.

Waiting behind the unfinished railroad bed to open upon the lost Federal regiments were the brigades of Col. Marcellus Douglass and Brig. Gen. Isaac Trimble. The distance between the opposing lines shrunk to under 100 yards when, "within a few paces of them, [Confederates] sprang up from their ambush, and with a wild yell poured a deadly volley full into our faces." Milroy's 5th West Virginia quickly fled the field. The 82nd Ohio was also staggered by the withering blast of musket fire. Their colonel, James Cantwell, was able to keep his regiment together, redress his lines, and continue to push forward. They reached the Confederate line and pushed through it in an area known as the "Dump," where a 100-yard gap existed in Jackson's line.

General Lawton sent in troops to push the Buckeyes out of the Confederate rear and to seal the gap in their line. When Lawton's troops and the Ohioans finally met, the weight of the Confederate counterattack was undeniable on Cantwell's Ohioans. The Ohio colonel himself was killed during the melee, and between the amount of fire they received and the death of their colonel, the regiment retreated.

This picture, taken from Jackson's line not far from Deep Cut, shows the approach route for many Federal attacks on August 29 and 30. (dw)

General Milroy tried to renew his assault on this sector of the Confederate line. The 3rd West Virginia advanced to within 150 feet from the Confederate line before the Rebels opened upon them. The overwhelming fire forced the regiment to "beat a hasty retreat." Milroy's cost in the morning fighting was 330 men.

The fighting across Sigel's front since his first cannon shots echoed loudly across the plains of Manassas nearly four hours earlier had taken a significant toll on his command. Casualties were extremely high, particularly in Brig. Gen. Carl Schurz's division. Just past the mid-day hour, however, Sigel was able to acknowledge that he had fulfilled his orders of the 28th to attack the enemy at dawn. His attack encompassed a mile-long front and had, it seemed to Sigel, pinned Jackson in place. Pope's chance to isolate and defeat Jackson before Lee and Longstreet arrived seemed to be working when John Pope finally arrived on the battlefield.

Pope placed his headquarters just east of Sudley Road, north of the Warrenton Pike, and near a rise of ground north of the Stone House known as Buck Hill.

Born near Steubenville, Ohio in 1810, James Cantwell served as a lieutenant in the 3rd Ohio Infantry during the Mexican-American War. He later served in the Ohio House of Representatives for one term before the war. He died of a gunshot wound to the head during the battle on August 29. (aohc)

The "Dump" has been described in various ways since the battle of Second Manassas, including using words such as "ravine," "gap," and "low point," while all give different measurements of its size, ranging from 50-75 yards. A byproduct of the unfinished railroad, it was a weak point in Jackson's line briefly penetrated by the 82nd Ohio. (kp)

Prussian-born Brig. Gen. Carl Schurz was also caught up in the 19th century revolutions in Europe. He was forced from Prussia to Switzerland, France to England, and finally emigrated to the United States in 1852. A strong anti-slavery Republican and Lincoln supporter, as well as a favorite among German northerners, Lincoln gave him a brigadier generalship in the spring of 1862. (loc)

There, Pope received a message from Sigel, which stated the condition of his corps and its need to be replaced. Pope informed Sigel that he had to hold on; there were simply no reinforcements to replace his worn regiments. Pope assured his subordinate, however, that there would not be another attack ordered from the Federal right until Porter and McDowell attacked Jackson's right flank and rear, which should happen at any moment. Sigel would have to hold the front lines of the Federal right in the meantime and resupply his men the best he could. Unfortunately, there was a miscommunication in one of Sigel's divisions, which resulted in a needless, piecemeal attack against the Confederate left.

General Lee wanted nothing more than to get at the "miscreant" Pope upon the completion of Longstreet's deployment. When Lee and Longstreet met to discuss the matter, however, Longstreet advised caution and patience, and, most importantly, a reconnaissance. The news, according to Longstreet, was not favorable for an immediate attack. He informed Lee that Pope's line extended well south of the Warrenton Turnpike, and, to attack this line, he would have to shift his deployment further to the right. At the same time, intelligence came into Longstreet's headquarters about a Federal force at Manassas Junction of unknown strength. If Longstreet shifted his men further to the right to attack Pope's left and rear, his own attacking column would expose its right and rear to this Federal force coming from the direction of the junction.

Lee was unhappy with this report. Still eager to get Longstreet's wing into the fight, and to come to Jackson's aid, Lee ordered his engineer staff at headquarters to perform their own reconnaissance. Before Lee could get them in the field, however, General Stuart reported that there was indeed a Federal column moving up the Manassas-Gainesville Road toward Longstreet's right. Without gathering further intelligence on this threat, no movement against Pope's left could be made. Jackson would continue to fight it out on his own hook. He would not have to wait long for the next Federal effort against his lines.

*   *   *

John Pope had been on the battlefield for nearly two hours. It was now 2 p.m. The afternoon was

This much-ignored monument today, erected by the Haymarket Agricultural Club, marks the location where generals Lee, Longstreet, and Jackson met around 12:30 p.m. on August 29. (dw)

fading away. If Pope was to move against Jackson again, he needed to get orders passed down the chain of command quickly and his units moving forward. After assessing the situation on the battlefield, a process that took nearly two hours, the commanding general was ready to act.

Pope sent orders to Maj. Gen. Joseph Hooker, divisional commander in the III Corps of the Army of the Potomac, to advance on Jackson's position. Hooker demurred, not wanting to make a frontal assault alone on such a strong position. Hooker asked Pope for additional units to make attacks simultaneously on Jackson's flanks to lessen the pressure that would be placed on his attack. He suggested Kearny's division as a reinforcing column and the Confederate left flank as its point of attack. Hooker's request for cooperation and support never materialized, though, and his men went forward alone.

Not long after Hooker received his orders, Pope ordered General Reno's units forward. This extra pressure along Jackson's front would keep "Stonewall" occupied while McDowell's corps arrived and went in on Jackson's right flank. Meanwhile, General Porter's V Corps had already arrived on the field, and in consultation with General McDowell, he established defensive positions opposite Longstreet's line. Having Porter and McDowell beyond Jackson's right was exactly what Pope wanted. But Pope believed that Porter would go straight into battle upon his arrival per the earlier Joint Orders. Porter did not, and thus Pope waited for an attack that would not come.

The sounds of battle echoing across the plains of Manassas continued to frustrate Robert E. Lee that afternoon. For a second time that day, Lee consulted with Longstreet about the merits of an attack on the

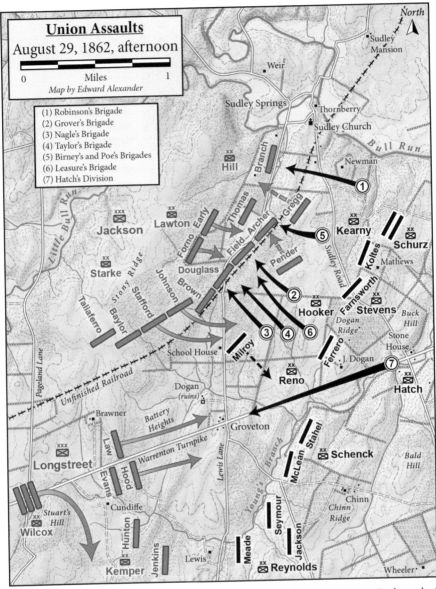

Union Assaults

August 29, 1862, afternoon

0   Miles   1

Map by Edward Alexander

(1) Robinson's Brigade
(2) Grover's Brigade
(3) Nagle's Brigade
(4) Taylor's Brigade
(5) Birney's and Poe's Brigades
(6) Leasure's Brigade
(7) Hatch's Division

UNION ASSAULTS, AUGUST 29, 1862, AFTERNOON—Pope continued to expect an attack against Jackson's right as he threw more attacks at Jackson's line on the afternoon of August 29. By that time, though, the situation had changed as Longstreet's portion of the army had arrived and blocked any Federal attack against Jackson's flank.

Federal left. Longstreet was able to determine that the force that arrived earlier opposite his front was not as strong as previously thought, and that an attack made on its flank was more than doable for his command. However, more dust clouds rose in the distance, from the areas of Bristoe Station and Manassas, which indicated not only more Federal reinforcements on the march to the battlefield, but also toward Longstreet's position. This intelligence, as well as some of his own observations, convinced Lee and Longstreet to shore up the army's right flank. Brigadier General Cadmus Wilcox's brigades were thus ordered to move from their position on the left of Longstreet's line to the right. Although Lee still wanted to attack, he acquiesced to Longstreet's hesitancy.

While the afternoon progressed, those same sounds that met Lee's ears also met Pope's. It was nearly 4 p.m., and the sound of battle had not grown, indicating Porter's expected attack still had not gone forward. Another thirty minutes ticked by. Pope's blood boiled at Porter's inaction. The general had a new order drawn up and sent to Porter at 4:30 p.m. "Your line of march brings you in on the enemy's right flank. I desire you to push forward into action at once on the enemy's flank, and, if possible on his rear," Pope ordered. Sadly for the Federal effort at Manassas, Porter did not receive this order until darkness almost consumed the battlefield. In anticipation of Porter's attack, Pope ordered General Heintzelman to move against Jackson's left flank. Heintzelman selected Kearny's division to fulfill Pope's order.

To the frustration of many high-ranking Union officers on the Federal right flank, Kearny's division had sat mostly idle throughout the day. Now, Brig. Gen. John C. Robinson's brigade and elements of Brig. Gen. David B. Birney's brigade went forward to assault Jackson's left. Kearny ordered the lead regiments of the attack, the 63rd and 105th Pennsylvania Infantry, to "give the enemy a fire and charge them, and endeavor to drive them from their position on the railroad."

The 63rd committed three separate charges against this portion of the Confederate line without much success and at frightful losses. To their right, however, two New York regiments from Birney's brigade were making far better progress.

When the 101st New York went into the fight, Kearny himself saw the regiment into action, calling

Dismissed from West Point during his second year, Brig. Gen. John C. Robinson has been described as a "salty old regular," and "the hairiest general . . . in a much-bearded army." He was still able to secure a commission in the Old Army despite his dismissal, served in Mexico, and slowly rose through the ranks in the prewar army. In April 1861, he was in command at Fort McHenry during the riots that plagued Baltimore. (loc)

Theodore Ayrault Dodge
received a privileged
education overseas in Berlin,
London, and Heidelberg,
during which he studied the
art of war. Dodge returned
to the United States in 1861
and immediately enlisted as a
private in the 101st New York
Infantry and, in 1862, accepted
an appointment as lieutenant
in the 119th New York Infantry.
He was wounded at Chantilly
on September 1. (nes)

out "Now boys, do your duty!" Theodore Ayrault Dodge of the regiment later wrote that Kearny's words "made our blood thrill and steeled our courage."

While Kearny's men moved forward, A. P. Hill was in conversation with Jackson's staffer Henry Kyd Douglas. Gregg's South Carolinians alone had been under fire for almost ten hours and had lost upwards of 500 men so far in the day's battle. In addition to the loss of men, those who were left were dangerously low on ammunition. Currently, Hill had details of men "out on the field collecting cartridges from the boxes of the dead and wounded—friend and foe." Hill asked Douglas "to ride to General Jackson and explain the situation and say, if he was attacked again, he would do the best he could, but could hardly hope for success."

Douglas was shocked by Hill's admission and rode to Jackson to deliver the message. Once relayed, worry appeared on Jackson's face. Jackson sent Douglas on his way back to Hill with the following message: "Tell him if they attack him again he must beat them."

Apprehension so consumed Jackson that he rode off after Douglas. Both men came across Hill, who was so worried about the condition of his brigades, he had ridden off in search of Jackson shortly after he had sent Douglas. Hill repeated his concerns to Jackson now in person. "General, your men have done nobly; if you are attacked again you will beat the enemy," "Stonewall" responded. This exchange was interrupted by a roar of musketry fire emanating from Hill's front. "Here it comes," yelled Hill as he turned his horse and galloped back towards his command. Jackson yelled after him "I'll expect you to beat them."

Kearny's assault slammed into Hill's front line. The attack was too much for the men of Maxcy Gregg's and Edward Thomas's brigades. Lieutenant Colonel Nelson A. Gesner, commanding the 101st New York, wrote "The enemy could not stand the charge but broke and fled." The gap that existed between these two brigades, the weakest point of Hill's line, was ably exploited by this Federal attack.

The New Yorkers' charge pushed the Confederates back into the railroad where "the enemy [was] so well entrenched in their well chosen rifle pit [and] showed no sign of giving away, we resorted to cold steel to drive them out." Pacing his line at the height of this latest attack, General Gregg continually implored, "Let us die here, my men, let us die here."

With the help of other Confederate regiments in the area, and a fighting tenacity yet unseen in the war, Gregg and Thomas were able to throw these Federals of Kearny's division out of the breach and seal it once more. Kearny's two brigades were in combat for less than forty minutes.

Birney's and Robinson's brigades were not alone in the fight. Supporting these brigades on the left were reinforcements from the IX Corps, Brig. Gen. Isaac Stevens's division. Around 5 p.m., orders reached Col. Daniel Leasure to advance his brigade to the right to assist with Kearny's attack. When Leasure's two regiments arrived to the left of Kearny's front line, Hazard Stevens, son of the division commander, reported with them to Kearny. Looking at Stevens, Kearny asked, "Will these men fight?" Stevens responded, "By God, General Kearny, these are my Roundheads!" in reference to the 100th Pennsylvania.

Asking to speak with their commander, Stevens gestured toward Colonel Leasure. Kearny rode up to Leasure, pointed toward the Confederate line, and said, "That is your line of advance, and sweep everything before you. Look out for your left; I'll take care of your right."

"We did so and drove them back," Pvt. Christopher Lobingier, Company A, 100th Pennsylvania noted in his diary entry for August 29. Lobingier continued, "This was the first charge I ever had a hand in and I hope it may be the last."

Leasure's fight quickly grew in intensity as Confederate reinforcements raced into the front lines. The added weight was too much for Leasure's small, two-regiment brigade. The fire of Leasure's brigade forced a momentary pause of the Confederate advance, enough time to allow his brigade to move rearward.

When Kearny's division went forward at 4 p.m., General Reno received orders to send Col. James Nagle's 1,500-man brigade of the IX Corps forward, as well. Pope's initial orders to Reno were to clear out the Confederate sharpshooters that were annoying Federal artillery in this area of the line. The position of Nagle's brigade on the field, and thus his route of advance, took him directly toward the center of Jackson's line of battle. Captain Oliver C. Bosbyshell of the 48th Pennsylvania recalled the brigade's advance: "Off we moved, over a clear field, to quite a dense wood, out of which we were to drive the rebels. The wood was skirted by a fence, which we

Posted to construction and repair of coastal defenses in New England following his graduation from West Point, Brig. Gen. Isaac Stevens served with distinction in the Mexican-American War. He later served as the governor of the Washington Territory and the elected territorial Congressional delegate. He saw action at Port Royal and Secessionville before being transferred to the Virginia theater under Pope. (loc)

Colonel Daniel Leasure, a native Pennsylvanian and graduate of Jefferson Medical College in Philadelphia, served in a three-month regiment before becoming colonel of the 100th Pennsylvania in August 1861. A prewar physician, he suffered a gunshot wound in the left leg during the fighting of August 29, 1862. (dw)

had scarcely crossed—in fact, our regiment was just getting over it—when bang! bang! whiz! whiz! and the battle commenced."

To the 48th's left, the men of the 6th New Hampshire also "received a terrific volley, which seemed to come from the ground just in front of us." When they crested the embankment, they "poured into them such a volley that they got out of their hiding-place on the double-quick, and retreated to the clearing and woods beyond." The charge of Nagle's brigade caught many Confederates in the railroad embankment by surprise with how quickly these Federals had advanced under intense musket fire.

Nagle's attack slammed into General Lawton's front, as well as Brig. Gen. Charles Field's brigade. Despite holding their fire until Nagle's regiments were within a few yards of the railroad cut before they delivered a devastating volley, the brigade's 500-yard attacking front was too much for the battle-weary Confederates. Not only did the men from Maryland, New Hampshire, and Pennsylvania reach the cut and force the Confederate defenders out of it, Nagle's regiments pursued them another 100 yards west of it. Seeing the collapse of his front line, Lawton sent in Col. Henry Forno's Louisianans to shore up Field's flagging Virginians. General Starke also sent in reinforcements to bolster Lawton's right flank. The Confederate counterattack struck Nagle's men in the front and lapped around their flanks.

The stark realization of being surrounded and cut off by Confederate infantry was enough for the officers across Nagle's brigade to give the order to retreat. "This we did in good order, returning fire for fire, and we got out in the clearing again," Bosbyshell wrote. Unfortunately for Nagle's men, reinforcements sent to him arrived too late.

General Milroy ordered an artillery battery pushed forward to support Nagle's brigade, though it failed to slow the Confederate attack, or the rout of Nagle's brigade and the reinforcements sent to him. Ultimately, this battery lost two of its guns. In the end, the latest Federal attacks of August 29, 1862, were defeated.

Across Jackson's left and center, the sounds of battle crested and trailed off. General Hill, whose men had once again thwarted any effort by the Federals to break through their line, dashed off a staff officer back to Jackson, who rode up to "Stonewall": "General Hill presents his compliments and says the attack of the enemy was repulsed."

"Tell him I knew he would do it," Jackson replied to Hill's staff officer. As Jackson's staffer Douglas later wrote, "This ended Jackson's fighting for the day."

But not Lee's.

* * *

General Lee still wanted Longstreet to make an assault against Pope's left flank. By the time Longstreet and Lee met to discuss the current situation on the field and the ability to attack, the tactical situation on the Federal left had changed drastically. The sounds of Federal infantry and artillery had crested and ebbed. General McDowell was pulled toward the Federal center and right, leaving only General Porter's V Corps in Longstreet's front. "Old Pete" estimated Porter's strength at 9,000, which provided Longstreet a tactical advantage in numbers. It seemed like the perfect opportunity to finally get Longstreet's wing into the fight.

Lee "again became anxious to bring on the battle by attacking down the Groveton Pike." But, as earlier, Longstreet was not on board. "I suggested that, the day being far spent, it might be as well to advance just before night upon a forced reconnaissance, get our troops in the most favorable positions, and have all things ready for battle at daylight the next morning," Longstreet said to Lee. Once again, Lee "reluctantly gave consent, and our plans were laid accordingly."

Longstreet rode off shortly after 6 p.m. to get the reconnaissance in motion. The general tapped Brig. Gen. John B. Hood's division to make the move. As Hood's preparations were completed, Federal infantry and artillery arrived on his front. The retreat of some of the front-line units on Jackson's left had convinced Pope that "Stonewall" was in fact retreating entirely from the field. With McDowell's corps now fully at hand to draw from, Pope ordered him to march King's division, now under command of Brig. Gen. John Hatch, along the Warrenton Turnpike, and to "fall upon the enemy, who was retreating toward the pike from the direction of Sudley Springs."

It was also at this time that McDowell shared vital information, some of which he had held nearly all day. First was a message from Brig. Gen. John Buford. The cavalryman had reported to McDowell at approximately 9:30 a.m. that a large enemy force

A paperhanger and painter by trade, when the war with Mexico broke out James Nagle and the company of artillery that he raised in 1842 were ready. Following the conflict, he returned to those professions and added sheriff to his resume. After the expiration of the three-month regiment, Nagle raised the 48th Pennsylvania Infantry. (na)

(Longstreet's) was then marching through Gainesville toward the battlefield and Pope's left. The second piece of information McDowell shared with Pope was more recent, only an hour old. It was a dispatch from V Corps commander Fitz John Porter. McDowell said the dispatch, from 6 p.m., informed him that Porter was still unsure of what to do with his command. Pope, still not knowing Porter had not received his orders from 4:30 p.m., was furious. Now, at 8:50 p.m., Pope ordered Porter to march his whole "command to the field of battle, and to report to me in person for orders." Pope added, "You are to understand that you are expected to comply strictly with this order, and to be present on the field within three hours after its reception or after daybreak tomorrow morning." There would be no flank attack made against the Confederate line by Porter that evening.

Meanwhile, back along Longstreet's front, the fading light provided a backdrop to the scene of new fighting on the Manassas battlefield. The weight of the Confederate reconnaissance in force was applied solely south of the Warrenton Turnpike. Hood recalled in his memoirs, "Onward they charged, driving the foe through field and forest, from position after position." This was not what Brig. Gen. John Hatch expected to find. As a matter of fact, just a short time earlier, before Hatch led his New Yorkers and sharpshooters forward, McDowell had yelled to Hatch as he rode away, "General Hatch, the enemy is in full retreat! Pursue him rapidly!"

Theron W. Haight, a first lieutenant in the 24th New York Infantry, said in 1895 that "the crack of musketry in front of us, and almost in our faces, informed us that we had been mistaken in the nature of the work to be performed. Instead of pursuing a flying enemy, we had been brought into a place where we must act on the defensive."

While the fight grew, darkness increased and Hood "discovered that my line was in the midst of the enemy; the obscurity of the night, which was deepened by a thick wood, made it almost impossible to distinguish friend from foe." Lieutenant Haight said of this moment in the battle, "Men were falling on all sides, and our line formation was practically lost. We were a mob, whose only unity was in blazing away at the line of fire at our front." Having committed three brigades into the fight, the Confederate line had more support nearby and still overlapped Hatch's left flank.

After twenty minutes of fighting, "I was forced to give the order for a retreat," Hatch wrote in his battle report. Hood's reconnaissance was over.

The news was not good for either Longstreet or Lee. The purpose of Hood's advance was to find and select a position from which to attack the Federal left flank the following morning. Hood, however, wrote that he "was unable to select a position and form upon it" because of the darkness and intermingling of the Federal and Confederate lines. He now rode to the rear in search of Lee and Longstreet to report the situation. Not only did Hood report about the condition on the field, but he also advised against an attack from his front in the morning. General Wilcox did as well, separately.

Longstreet ordered the two generals' commands back to where they had jumped off earlier that evening, and the morning attack for August 30 was canceled. Lee could only hope that his adversary would provide him another opportunity to be subdued the following day.

"The battle of the 29th was over," wrote Alfred Lee of the 82nd Ohio Infantry. "Its conclusion left us in possession of the field and of part of the ground which had been wrested from the enemy, but that was all. In the main object we had failed, and a golden opportunity had been missed."

Titled "Collecting the Wounded," this scene depicts the aftermath of the fighting of August 29, 1862. Warren Lee Goss wrote in *Century Magazine* in 1886, "[S]o soon as the fighting ceased, many sought without orders to rescue comrades lying wounded between the opposing lines. There seemed to be an understanding between the men of both armies that such parties were not to be disturbed in their mission of mercy." (b&l)

THE WISCONSIN COMPANY
1st REGIMENT of BERDANS
U. S. SHARPSHOOTERS
used many cartridges on this
spot, August 30, 1862 - losing
1 man killed and 8 wounded.

Position marked by GEO. E. ALBEE, a private of the company

Pandemonium Made Real

CHAPTER NINE
AUGUST 30, 1862, MORNING–
MID-AFTERNOON

"The morning broke upon the Confederates brightly, finding them in position of night before," remembered Sgt. George Wise in the 17th Virginia. For many, the silence that morning falsely suggested the battle had come to a conclusion. Sergeant Wise was one of them. "Not a sound broke the stillness of the morning & many thought that the enemy had fallen back," he said of the morning of August 30.

While these Confederates whiled away the quiet of the morning, both Lee and Pope took the opportunity to compose updates to their respective superiors: Lee to Confederate President Jefferson Davis and Pope to Maj. Gen. Henry Halleck.

Lee felt that the campaign by August 30 "ha[d] succeeded in deceiving the enemy as to its object," drawing Pope and the Army of Virginia away from the Rappahannock. To capitalize on these gains, Lee wrote to Davis, "We have no time to lose & must make every exertion if we expect to reap advantage."

To General Halleck in Washington, Pope wrote, "We fought a terrific battle here yesterday with the combined forces of the enemy, which lasted with continuous fire from daylight until dark." The commander of the Army of Virginia even asserted to Halleck that by darkness on August 29, "the enemy was driven from the field which we now occupy." Although his army had sustained casualties of "not less than 8,000 men" in the previous day's battle and, according to Pope, Jackson's casualties were at

Federal troops had to advance uphill toward the distant treeline over open ground in the face of Confederate artillery and infantry fire during their assault against the Deep Cut on the afternoon of August 30, 1862. (kp)

An 1884 drawing of the Deep Cut based on a wartime sketch. (b&l)

least twice that number, he now had Jackson on the precipice of defeat. One final blow should be all that was needed to force Jackson to retreat and for Pope to claim victory on the doorstep of the nation's capital.

As Pope continued to write to Halleck, he was interrupted by the arrival of intelligence confirming his belief in Jackson's intention to withdraw from the battlefield. "The news just reaches me that the enemy is retreating toward the mountains," he jotted down in real time to Halleck, "and I go forward at once to see."

Pope moved out from his headquarters on Buck Hill and, with his headquarters entourage, went forward to confirm this latest information. Once at the front, "Pope found the enemy still in front of him," Col. David H. Strother wrote. Yet, somehow, Pope interpreted what he saw as confirmation that Jackson was in retreat. Pope headed back toward his headquarters and summoned his top-ranking officers

A drawing depicts Starke's brigade fighting with stones near the "Deep Cut." (b&l)

to meet him there to discuss his findings and lay out the day's strategy. The time was 7:00 a.m.

There was great confusion in the council that morning between Pope's report to his officers and the reality of the situation on the ground. Major General Samuel P. Heintzelman noted, "There were great doubts about the position of the enemy." Astonishingly, despite the doubt and confusion of Jackson's line, his intentions, and the whereabouts of Longstreet's column, the council decided to attack Jackson's left flank near Sudley Church with the commands of Heintzelman, McDowell, and Maj. Gen. Fitz John Porter from the Army of the Potomac.

As the details of the attack were finalized and the various unit commanders filtered away from army headquarters to return to their commands and prepare them for the day's planned actions, General Porter arrived. He carried vital intelligence that should have greatly altered the plan that Pope and the council had decided upon. Porter informed Pope that Jackson's line was extended beyond Pope's left south of the Warrenton Turnpike by the arrival of Longstreet's corps the previous day—intelligence Pope still would not or could not accept.

Few spoke up in support of Porter's report and the possible consequences of the pending threat, and the news made little difference in Pope's mind. His strategic and tactical plans for the day were already set, his orders to his attacking columns written in proverbial stone—all based upon his unwillingness to accept that Longstreet's column was present on the field and on his army's left flank and rear.

Staff officers continued to arrive at Pope's headquarters with updated information from the front as the morning continued to pass. Still believing that Jackson was retreating, Pope could not understand why the Confederates remained in his front. Pope took no aggressive action to find out or validate his line of reasoning. Instead, Pope and McDowell "spent the morning under a tree waiting for the enemy to retreat," while another staff officer believed that Pope's actions and speech around headquarters that morning demonstrated that he was "wholly at a loss what to do and what to think."

At Lee's headquarters that morning, Lee, Jackson, Longstreet, and Stuart also did not understand Pope's passivity. Lee sought counsel from his officers on the next course of action. Still eager to attack Pope with

THE WISCONSIN COMPANY
1st REGIMENT of BERDANS
U. S. SHARPSHOOTERS
used many cartridges on this
spot, August 30, 1862-losing
1 man killed and 8 wounded.
Position marked by GEO. E. ALBEE, a private of the company

Only 17 years old in August 1862, Pvt. George E. Albee and his comrades of the 1st United States Sharpshooters formed the skirmish line that preceded Porter's attack. Albee was wounded in the fight but survived. He later received the Medal of Honor for actions performed during the Indian Wars. After the war, Albee returned to the Manassas battlefield and erected this marker which sat on a cedar post. The original marker has since been replaced and faithfully reproduced by the National Park Service, though today's marker stands in the historical location of Albee's original. (kp)

Longstreet's column, Lee finally settled on remaining on the defensive to await Pope's next movement. The decision to remain on the defensive left the officers "a little apprehensive that Pope was going to get away from us," recalled Longstreet in a postwar memoir.

After the meeting broke up, while Jackson rode back toward his command, he passed by his old brigade, the Stonewall Brigade, now under the leadership of Col. William S. H. Baylor. Baylor had only been in command of the brigade for three weeks. As Jackson rode by the prewar lawyer from Virginia, he called out, "Well Baylor, it looks as if there will be no fight today . . . ."

By mid-day, as Porter worked to get his command and those assigned to support him into position to attack Jackson's left, Pope called it off. He still erroneously believed that Jackson's command was retreating westward. Convinced of this notion, Pope now ordered Porter's corps to "push forward on the Warrenton Turnpike, followed by the divisions of Brigadier General Rufus King and Reynolds. The division of Brigadier General Ricketts will pursue the Haymarket Road, followed by the corps of Major General Heintzelman." Pope placed McDowell in charge "of the pursuit."

Nearing noon, General Reynolds informed Pope that Longstreet's wing of the Confederate army was indeed on the field. It not only had a strong position beyond the army's left flank, but also stretched toward its rear. Yet again Pope dismissed reality and refused to cancel Porter's movement. Instead, for the next several hours, Porter worked to get more than 20,000 men of his corps, and that of Brig. Gens. John Hatch's and John Reynolds's divisions, in position for a pursuit of Jackson's retreating soldiers. In reality, the preparations for this pursuit transitioned into preparations for an assault against the stalwart defenders of Jackson's line of battle. By 3:00 p.m., with preparations completed, Porter's column moved forward.

Although General McDowell had assembled a large assaulting force built around Porter's corps, not all of these units would be brought to bear along the Confederate front. On Porter's right flank, McDowell had added his own corps' first division under General

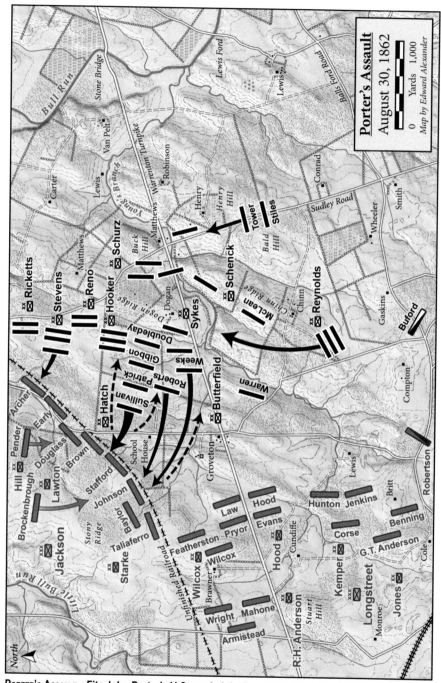

Porter's Assault
August 30, 1862

Map by Edward Alexander

0   Yards 1,000

PORTER'S ASSAULT—Fitz John Porter's V Corps led the largest Federal attack of the battle on the afternoon of August 30. It was repulsed and caused Irvin McDowell to move Federal troops north of the Warrenton Turnpike, setting up disaster for Pope's army.

Hatch. Adding more weight to the far right of the Federal attack were several brigades from the first division of the IX Corps. Although their commanding officer, Brig. Gen. Isaac Stevens, was not ordered to do so, he deployed these brigades in an attack in-depth on his own initiative. General Reynolds's division of Pennsylvania Reserves were still in motion toward Porter's left. Out of all of these units—more than 20,000 soldiers—fewer than half actually went into the assault that afternoon.

Further handicapping the effectiveness of Porter's attack was the loss of some of his units and higher-ranking officers. Following orders that were given earlier on August 30, V Corps division commander Maj. Gen. George W. Morell marched away from the battlefield with his own brigade and a reserve brigade toward Centreville. Their replacements would be new to their posts just hours before they would lead their men into combat. This created a command vacuum within the V Corps. Terrain, poor leadership, an exposed, dangling left flank, and the fact that Porter attacked into the apex of the junction of Longstreet's and Jackson's wings meant that Porter's assault, commanded by McDowell, was doomed almost from the start—an attack that proved to be the largest Union assault of the battle.

The attack moved forward regardless. First, Federal skirmishers pushed out of the Groveton Woods, across Groveton-Sudley Road, and toward a dry creek bed. The skirmish line soon needed more help, but the exposed men had to wait nearly 30 minutes for assistance.

The units that led the right of Porter's attack were the 24th and 30th New York. After clearing the woods, they had some 350 yards of open ground to cover before reaching the Confederate line. They came under fire immediately. To Theron Haight of the 24th, the advance "seemed like the popular

Edwin Forbes depicted some of the Federal infantry on the left of Porter's assault. (loc)

Completed just weeks after the closing scenes of the Civil War, the Groveton Monument was dedicated on June 11, 1865. Erected in honor of the Federal dead of Second Manassas, it is located near the "Deep Cut" of the Unfinished Railroad. (dw)

idea of pandemonium made real, and indeed it is scarcely too much to say that we were transformed for the time from a lot of good-natured boys to the most bloodthirsty of demoniacs." The New Yorkers continued to push forward. When they finally reached the railroad embankment, the 24th New York's Maj. Andrew Jackson Barney dug his spurs into his horse and bolted atop the embankment. A bullet soon struck Barney in the head. Toppled from his horse, the dead major lay atop the embankment.

The New Yorkers looked toward their rear in vain for support. The fire was so intense that the next wave of Federal reinforcements could not make it to the embankment. Colonel Leroy Stafford's Louisianans held the embankment that Col. Timothy Sullivan's brigade attacked. The Louisiana soldiers, who initially poured deadly volleys into Sullivan's ranks, soon ran low on ammunition. Men frantically searched their dead and wounded comrades' cartridge boxes for more lead. Private Michael O'Keefe of the 1st Louisiana used a different tactic. "Boys, give them the rocks," he yelled. Haight recalled that there then

Andrew Jackson Barney was 32 years old when he enlisted in May 1861 in the 24th New York Infantry. A native of Massachusetts, the Barney family moved to New York where, in 1851, Barney's physician father invited Thomas Jonathan Jackson to recover his health. The family, and Andrew, became good friends with the future Confederate officer. (usda)

came "an unlooked for variation in the proceedings. Huge stones began to fall about us, and now and then one of them would happen to strike with very unpleasant effect." The Louisianans flung rocks for only a few moments before reinforcements arrived and drove Hatch's Yankees back across the open plain. The Federals had been stranded in their position for over 30 minutes.

On Sullivan's left, the men of Brig. Gen. Daniel Butterfield's division had 700 yards of ground to traverse under Confederate artillery fire before receiving volleys of musketry fire from Jackson's infantry. These V Corps men yelled out three cheers and then emerged from the Groveton Woods. Halfway to the unfinished railroad, bullets added to the artillery fire, causing the ground in front of the Confederate position to resemble "a mill pond in a shower." Roberts's men on the right of Butterfield's formation made it close to an excavated section of the railroad grade—later known as the Deep Cut—held by Col. Bradley Johnson's brigade, but were stymied by the wall of enemy fire before making it all the way there.

Weeks's men on Roberts's left, led by the 17th New York, struck an advanced regiment of Johnson's brigade, the 48th Virginia, and scattered it to the rear. The rest of Johnson's men held on and poured a deadly fire into Weeks's regiments. The hole left by the 48th Virginia's retreat still had to be plugged, though; William Starke turned to the Stonewall Brigade for this task.

The Stonewall Brigade held Starke's second line 200 yards behind the Deep Cut when Porter's attack began. Upon receiving orders to advance, the brigade came under long-range fire from the attacking Federals. The men staggered. Brigade commander William Baylor threw himself in front of the brigade line, grabbed the colors of the 33rd Virginia, and yelled, "Boys, follow me!" Almost immediately, Baylor was killed. The Virginians advanced over his body to the railroad cut, paying dearly for the advance across the open field. "The conflict from the woods to the railroad was terrible," one of the survivors recalled.

Jackson's men wrestled the upper hand back in this close-quarters fight. Porter considered adding more weight to his punch, but the Confederate artillery that had zeroed in on their advance precluded him from adding to the bloodshed. William Pender's brigade showed up to further buttress Starke's line, and the

Union troops could not break through. Defeated, the unhurt Federals brave enough to recross the open field in their rear peeled away from the railroad embankment. The largest Union assault of the battle ended 30 minutes after it began.

Irvin McDowell watched Porter's withdrawal with trepidation. He feared that the repulse set the stage for a powerful Confederate counterattack by Jackson's men. Thus, he made the momentous decision to move Brig. Gen. John Reynolds's three Pennsylvania brigades off Chinn Ridge and send them north of the Warrenton Turnpike to support Porter's line on Dogan Ridge.

Once the two lead brigades of Reynolds's division crossed the pike, the sound of shooting grew in intensity south of the road.

A pre-war boot and shoe maker, Col. Timothy Sullivan was born in Ireland. A resident of Oswego, New York, he entered Federal service in May 1861 as colonel of the 24th New York Infantry. (loc)

For My Country and the Old Flag

CHAPTER TEN

AUGUST 30, 1862, LATE AFTERNOON

Jackson's line had once again bent but not broken under the weight of renewed Union attacks. However, the sheer size of Porter's assault rendered many of the front-line troops in Jackson's command combat ineffective. Although they had done all that had been asked of them, they and Jackson needed help. For the first time in the campaign, Jackson sent for aid.

Lee immediately sent orders to Longstreet to send a division to Jackson. Longstreet realized sending a division to Jackson would take time, something Jackson did not have. Instead, Longstreet ordered Hood's division forward into the fight, while Col. Stephen D. Lee's guns, eighteen in all and located at the Brawner Farm, continued to rain lead and iron among Porter's retreating masses. Now near 4:00 p.m., Longstreet's orders to Hood were "to push for the plateau at the Henry House, in order to cut off retreat at the crossings of Young's Branch."

Longstreet's assault included the three divisions of Brig. Gens. John B. Hood, James L. Kemper, and David R. Jones. In the initial moments of the attack, Union artillery immediately opened fire. The incessant rain of shells from Federal batteries posted both north and south of the Warrenton Turnpike slowed many regiments in the front ranks of Hood's line.

Hood's Texas Brigade made the first contact with the enemy. Positioned opposite their front, the 1,100 soldiers of Col. Gouverneur Warren's 5th and 10th New York Infantry, supported by Lt. Charles Hazlett's

This monument—dedicated in honor of the 5th New York in 1906 by the state—rests in the area where 124 men of the regiment were killed, including both color bearers and 7 of 8 of the color guard, and 223 wounded. Their losses occurred in just a matter of moments on August 30. (dw)

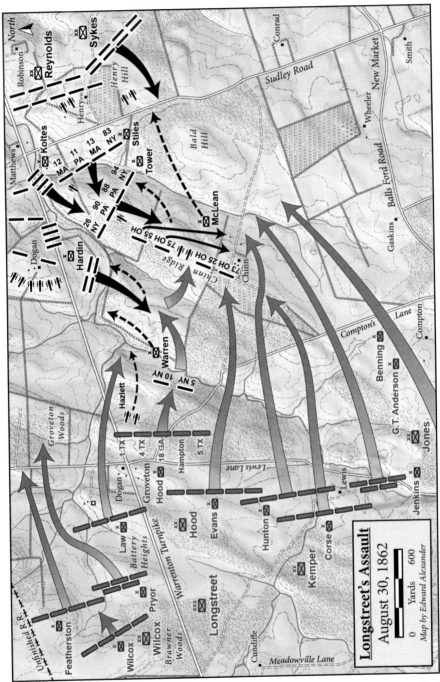

LONGSTREET'S ASSAULT—In approximately three hours, James Longstreet's counterattack pushed the Army of Virginia to the brink of destruction. Determined fighting by Federals on Chinn Ridge and along Sudley Road allowed Pope's army to escape across Bull Run on the night of August 30.

Battery D, 5th U.S. Artillery, were all that stood between Hood and Henry Hill.

We "rushed forward at a charge from the word go, all the time keeping up an unearthly yell," a soldier in the 18th Georgia recalled. Arriving at a distance of less than 100 yards from Warren's main line, each side delivered devastating volleys of fire. Private Andrew Coats in the 5th New York noted, "For a short time the Regiment tried to fight back the overwhelming force that was pouring in a fearful stream of destruction and death upon it, but the stream became a torrent, as the right and left flanks of the enemy almost surrounded us." Of the carnage the Texas Brigade inflicted on the New Yorkers, Coats continued, "War has been designated as Hell, and I can assure you that where the Regiment stood that day was the very vortex of Hell. Not only were men wounded, or killed, but they were riddled."

Gouverneur K. Warren graduated second in the West Point Class of 1850. Warren saw combat from the war's earliest days at Big Bethel as the lieutenant colonel of the 5th New York and ended the war commanding an army corps. (loc)

Warren realized this was a fight that his small brigade could not win. He tried in vain to have orders sent down the line to begin a fighting retreat, but the orders either could not be heard over the cacophony of the battle or were not received. Warren had to grab one of the 5th New York's flags and gesture it in a rearward motion to get his Zouaves to withdraw.

Among the retreating Zouaves was Pvt. James Webb of Company F, 5th New York. As he made his way rearward, Webb realized that the Confederate assault would take Hazlett's battery and decided to alert it to the danger on their left. Through a hail of bullets, some piercing his uniform and one creasing his side, the "forlorn hope of the most desperate character," as one Company E man described it, had been successful. Hazlett ordered the guns to limber up and escape their deadly predicament. Webb was later awarded the Medal of Honor for his actions that day.

But the day was far from over, and many more acts of gallantry and bravery had yet to transpire.

The first actions of Longstreet's assault were incredibly costly to Warren's brigade. The 5th New York alone lost 332 men out of the 525 they brought to the field the previous afternoon. Of those casualties, 120 were dead, the highest number of killed of any regiment on any Civil War battlefield. The 10th New York's reports submitted in the wake of the battle listed 21 killed, 65 wounded, and 27 missing. These staggering losses occurred over the length of just ten minutes of combat. Corporal Joseph B. Polley, 4th

Erected by the state of Texas during the battle's sesquicentennial, it "Remembers the valor and devotion of her soldiers who participated in the battle of Second Manassas, Virginia–August 28-30, 1862." (dw)

From Brooklyn, New York, James Webb was only 19 years old when he enlisted in Co. F, 5th New York Infantry in July 1861. A year later, at age 20, his heroism on August 30, 1862, was recognized with the Medal of Honor. His citation, in part, reads, "Under heavy fire Private Webb voluntarily carried information to a battery commander that enabled him to save his guns from capture. Was severely wounded, but refused to go to the hospital and participated in the remainder of the campaign." (wikip)

Texas Infantry, described "Looking up the hill," in their front, where "a strange and ghastly spectacle met our eyes. An acre of ground was literally covered with the dead, dying, and wounded of the Fifth New York Zouaves, the variegated colors of whose peculiar uniform gave the scene the appearance of a Texas hillside in spring, painted with wild flowers of every hue and color."

The Texas Brigade pursued the survivors vigorously. Down at the bottom of the hill, and in and around Young's Branch, Capt. William H. Sellers, a staff officer for Hood acting as the commander of Hood's brigade, struggled to get the brigade to stop and reform before resuming the offensive. Although its attack on Warren and Hazlett was successful, the speed at which the attack occurred coupled with the casualties they had sustained had thrown the brigade into immense confusion.

As the fighting waged between the New Yorkers and the Texans, the crescendo of the engagement reached McDowell's ears. He realized his earlier orders to abandon nearby Chinn Ridge and redeploy those troops elsewhere to be a mistake. Only a few sparse Federal troops now occupied the area—not nearly enough to stop Longstreet's assault, which was moving in that direction. McDowell was able to catch several of the units he had ordered away near the rear of their route of march and rush them back toward Warren's original position.

In the meantime, a hardy band of Buckeyes under the command of Col. Nathaniel C. McLean was all that stood atop the important position of Chinn Ridge. Originally, they had deployed on the ridge as support for John Reynolds's Pennsylvania Reserves. The Ohioans had not been there long before Reynolds received his orders from McDowell to march toward the center of the Federal line. McLean watched uncomfortably as the Pennsylvanians moved away and uncovered his

Alfred Waud, renowned Civil War sketch artist, drew the moment Warren's New Yorkers broke in the face of Longstreet's assault on August 30, 1862. (loc)

front. He ordered his brigade to advance to the military crest of Chinn Ridge and deploy. Once there, the Buckeyes watched in horror the ferocious Confederate attack of Hood's brigade that utterly destroyed Warren's New Yorkers and handily brushed aside Col. Martin Davis Hardin's Pennsylvania Reserve brigade. Further worry rippled through the lines of Ohioans as they noticed additional lines following up the front line of the assault.

As Hood's brigade cleared the woods in front of McLean's line, the Buckeyes unleashed a withering fire. Three regiments of Hood's brigade were literally pushed back into the woodlot by the weight of the Federal volley. In the coming moments, additional troops from Georgia and South Carolina arrived on the scene. The pressure on the few defenders on Chinn Ridge grew with each new arrival.

Erected by the state of New York in 1906, this monument honors the 10th New York Volunteer Regiment, and marks the area where they fought on August 30, 1862. Inscribed on the monument are the following words, "Braver men than those who fought and fell that day could not be found." (dw)

A hail of bullets and artillery fire raked the newly arrived 23rd South Carolina. Casualties among the regiment's officers mounted quickly. Both the colonel and lieutenant colonel were wounded and down before the regiment even cleared the woodlot. Finally in position at its edge, Maj. John Whilden ordered a charge toward the Ohioans' right flank. Once again, the Buckeyes held.

The 23rd's colors fell in the assault. Whilden picked them up, rallied his men, and led them forward in a second attempt to dislodge the right flank of McLean's brigade. He became the next officer casualty of the 23rd, wounded by five separate bullets. His death at the front of the regiment and the weight of the renewed fire by the Ohioans sent the 23rd back into the woods. In just these two separate movements against the Buckeyes, the 23rd South Carolina lost 149 men of the 250 they took into the attack. The attack and defense of Chinn Ridge was becoming a costly and bloody affair and stalled Longstreet's push toward the final objective of Henry Hill.

The relentless attacks of Longstreet's units against the beleaguered Federal left continued, though. While in the thick of the battle and holding his Ohio regiments together, McLean witnessed another line of Confederate infantry moving toward his position on Chinn Ridge. These men, part of Brig. Gen. James L. Kemper's division, moved quickly to support the

Colonel Nathaniel C. McLean's finest day in the Civil War was August 30, 1862, when his brigade stood against the first wave of Longstreet's assaults against Chinn Ridge. His father famously wrote the dissenting opinion for the Supreme Court when it heard the case of *Dred Scott v. Sandford*. (na)

James Kemper served as a captain during the Mexican-American War and settled in practicing law during the remainder of the antebellum years. He also served in the Virginia House of Delegates as its speaker, a chairman on several committees, and president of the board of visitors of the Virginia Military Institute. (loc)

stalled Confederate assault. In just ten minutes, Kemper's men forced the Ohioans to retreat.

Brigadier General Zealous B. Tower's brigade of Pennsylvanians and New Yorkers arrived and deployed on the eastern slope of Chinn Ridge behind the withdrawing Ohioans. Captain George Leppien's 5th Maine Battery also attempted to slow the Confederate advance. Additional regiments were then en route, as well as more Federal guns. Colonel John Stiles's brigade was not far behind.

General Tower and his men marched into a maelstrom. "The confusion among the troops on the hill was great; officers and men shouting, shells tearing through and exploding, the incessant rattle of muskets, the cries of the wounded—all combined made up a scene that was anything but encouraging," John Vautier, the regimental historian of the 88th Pennsylvania Infantry later remembered. Tower's brigade, like McLean's, was under immense fire from the ever-growing Confederate reinforcements. Lieutenant Colonel Joseph McLean in command of the 88th Pennsylvania was "severely wounded high up on the thigh, the ball rupturing the main artery." Lieutenant William J. Rannells of the 75th Ohio, who was near McLean when he was wounded, recalled what happened next. "With a strap the Lieut. Col. gave me I succeeded in stopping the hemorrhage of the wound," Rannells wrote to McLean's wife in the days after the battle. The letter detailed McLean's final moments. As Confederates approached the colonel, he ordered Rannells and the three men of the 88th that were helping him to the rear to drop him "and save yourselves, for I must die." When the three Keystoners dropped him, it "caused the strap to slip below the wound. It commenced to bleed as freely as ever." The fighting swirled around Rannells and McLean, the colonel wounded again in the same leg below the knee. Now a prisoner, Rannells later told McLean's wife, Elizabeth, that their captors "would not help me take him to some surgeon. They made me leave him, when he said, 'tell my wife she will never blush to be my widow. I die for my country and the old flag.'" McLean left a widow and seven children behind, a painful reminder of the cost of the war.

At the same time that the dramatic final moments of McLean's life played out, Vautier of the 88th wrote that "the yells of the combatants, the noise of the bursting shells, and the agonizing screams of

the wounded and the dying made the place perfect bedlam." Leppien's guns were overrun. Colonel John Stiles's brigade now advanced through the remnants of Tower's battered New Yorkers and Pennsylvanians. Over the course of the next 30 minutes, Stiles's mixed brigade of troops from Massachusetts, New York, and Pennsylvania faced ever-increasing pressure atop Chinn Ridge. The fighting was so severe that one 11th Pennsylvania soldier wrote, "Entire regiments seemed to melt away in an instant."

Casualties mounted among the Federals at Chinn Ridge at an alarming rate. The 11th Pennsylvania alone sustained nearly 240 casualties within the first minutes of its arrival to the fight. Officer casualties also soared. "General Towers [sic] was seriously wounded and taken from the field," while "Colonel Fletcher Webster, of the Twelfth Massachusetts, was among the early slain on the left." Fletcher was the eldest son of Daniel Webster, a well-known lawyer and politician during the first half of the nineteenth century.

The fighting was so close and chaotic between the two lines that in addition to enlisted and officer casualties, trophies of the battle were already being collected. "Samuel Coleman, private Company E, Seventeenth Virginia, in the hottest of the fight wrested from the hands of the color-sergeant of the Eleventh Pennsylvania Regiment his regimental colors and handed them to me," reported brigade commander Col. Montgomery Corse.

The Federal regiments on Chinn Ridge were in desperate need of support. Two more brigades dispatched by General Sigel were moving toward Chinn Ridge. By the time they arrived, so too had more reinforcements for the Confederate attack. Once again Longstreet's unrelenting attack on the defenders on the Federal left overlapped their flanks and applied

LEFT: **Brigadier General Zealous B. Tower graduated at the top of the West Point Class of 1841 and served on Winfield Scott's staff in the Mexican-American War alongside George McClellan and Robert E. Lee. Tower suffered a serious wound at Second Manassas and spent the remainder of the war as Superintendent of West Point and in the Western Theater.** (mitw)

CENTER: **William J. Rannells enlisted in the 75th Ohio Infantry in December 1861 at the age of 22. A lieutenant in Co. I, he was captured on August 30 on Chinn Ridge but soon exchanged. He was later wounded at Gettysburg and captured a second time at the battle of Gainesville, Florida in 1864.** (mollus)

RIGHT: **Born and raised in New York City, John Wesley Stiles was in the ship chandlery business before the war. Colonel of the 83rd New York Infantry, in January 1863 he was discharged for disability due to "the exposure and fatigue of the campaign to the Rapidan and subsequent battle of Bull Run."** (honr)

LEFT: Son of German immigrants and born in the United States, George Leppien was actually educated abroad for 14 years, including 5 spent at a Prussian military academy. By November 1861, he was appointed captain of the 5th Maine Battery. A stern "camp disciplinarian" and a "scientific and practical artillerist," his work in training his battery paid off in his absence on August 30, 1862, on top of Chinn Ridge. (loc)

CENTER: John D. Vautier enlisted in the 88th Pennsylvania Infantry in September 1861. Present for almost all the engagements the 88th participated in, he was wounded at Cold Harbor in 1864. He later became the regiment's historian, publishing the unit's official history in 1894. (hopa)

RIGHT: Colonel Fletcher Webster of the 12th Massachusetts stood in the shadow of his famous father Daniel. He made a career for himself working in the State Department before offering his services to Massachusetts and the United States during the Civil War. Webster had a premonition of his death on August 29, 1862. (loc)

extreme weight to their front. The two fresh brigades of Brig. Gen. David R. Jones's Confederate division were finally able to drive the Federal defenders off Chinn Ridge.

Standing in the way of complete Confederate control of the ridge and plateau, as well as a clear path toward Sudley Road, Henry Hill, and the center of Pope's army, were Sigel's reinforcements. Troops from Brig. Gen. Julius Stahel's brigade, and Cols. John Koltes and Wlodzimierz Krzyzanowski's brigades were all that stood between Longstreet and the destruction of the Army of Virginia.

The 41st New York charged ahead to retake the lost guns of Leppien's 5th Maine Battery. They "endeavored to save the cannons, but in vain," reported Col. Gustavus A. Muhleck of the 73rd Pennsylvania Volunteer Infantry. Colonel Koltes "rode up to the front of his brigade, and swinging his sword high in the air, while ordering his command to take that rebel battery," was killed by a shell fragment. His death only inspired the men in his brigade to once and for all recapture the guns and "A rush was made toward the rebel cannons. Some of my men . . . reached the pieces, but were unsupported [and] surrounded," wrote Muhleck.

The latest wave of Federal troops on Chinn Ridge fought on for another 30 minutes. Eventually, like those that attempted to hold it before them, the "small regiments, exhausted and decimated and unsupported, had in their turn to fall back." With their flanks overlapped and immense artillery and infantry in their front, it was a hopeless situation. The fight for Chinn Ridge waged for nearly 90 minutes at an immense cost to both Pope and Lee.

The cost to Lee was doubly heavy. Not only had Longstreet's wing been heavily battered during

The area in which McLean's brigade held off numerous attacks by Longstreet's units. The Ohioans were eventually pushed off the ridge, as well as their reinforcements. (dw)

its attack on Chinn Ridge, but the extended time it took to secure it and push on toward Henry Hill— Longstreet's true objective—placed the Confederate attack in a race against the fading daylight. The exorbitant Federal casualties at Chinn Ridge had bought Pope time to construct a new defensive line on his left. In total, Pope was able to deploy four brigades of infantry along Sudley Road by 6 p.m.

Meanwhile, as Longstreet's frontline units south of the Warrenton Pike made it to Chinn Ridge and engaged in heavy fighting, his units north of the pike did not immediately move into the battle. The array of Federal artillery supported by Federal infantry north of the pike on Dogan Ridge had, until that time, blocked any significant Confederate effort against it. Colonel Evander Law's brigade moved forward into the teeth of the Federal batteries atop the ridge.

The combination of effective infantry fire and Federal artillery booming with canister sent Law's men reeling. Law did not move forward again against

The 41st New York Infantry was raised as a three year regiment in June 1861. Nicknamed the De Kalb Regiment, the unit was composed mostly of men of German ethnicity, of whom many were veterans of the war between Prusssia and Denmark in the late 1840s and early 1850s. This image was taken by Civil War photographer Timothy O'Sullivan near Manassas in July 1862. (loc)

The 88th Pennsylvania Infantry became a family affair for the McLeans. George, Joseph McLean's brother, raised the regiment, and Joseph's son, Daniel, served as its drummer. George relinquished command of the regiment on August 25 to his brother Joseph due to illness. Joseph was killed leading it in battle on August 30. His remains were never recovered. (hopa)

Dogan Ridge until the Federals withdrew during the army's general retreat. Other Confederate units, later in the battle, would, however. Two brigades from Brig. Gen. Cadmus Wilcox's division capitalized on the retreat of Federal forces north of the pike. Making their way to Dogan Ridge, they captured eight Federal guns and numerous prisoners.

To the south, General D. R. Jones pushed on with his division toward the critical intersection of the Warrenton Turnpike and Sudley Road. This crossing was vital to the movements of Pope's army and, if captured, would not only bring the battle to an end for Pope, but also cut off a major line of retreat for the Federals.

Within several hundred yards of the road crossing, Federal artillery on Henry Hill opened on Jones's advance. At the same time, two brigades of General Reynolds's Pennsylvania Reserves moved forward and fired on Jones's flank and front.

Elements of the two all-Georgia brigades in Jones's command wheeled to meet this threat. For a brief moment, Confederate success against this new threat and the Sudley Road line seemed within grasp. Heavy fighting caused two of Reynolds's left-most regiments along Sudley Road, as well as regiments of General Milroy's brigade to their left, to break in the face of the Georgians' fire. "[W]e gained the road . . . [and] received orders to lie down and fire,"

Dedicated in 1914 by the survivors of the 12th Massachusetts, this monument marks the approximate area where Col. Webster was killed on August 30. The boulder was brought to the battlefield from Webster Place in Marshfield, Massachusetts. (dw)

Maj. P. J. Shannon of the 15th Georgia Infantry reported. Union reinforcements soon threatened the 15th's right flank. Although they were "ordered to fire by the right oblique, which we did with great havoc on the enemy," they were ultimately forced to fall back.

Help finally arrived for Jones's beleaguered Georgians when Maj. Gen. Richard H. Anderson's division deployed on Jones's right flank. Additional Confederate artillery was driven forward as well, and J. E. B. Stuart reached the front to deploy the guns. All these units now made a concentrated effort against the dangling left flank of Pope's Sudley Road position while more Confederates went forward on their right.

The Virginians in Brig. Gen. William Mahone's brigade overlapped the Federal flank and crossed Sudley Road itself. Their arrival on the flank of the Sudley Road line was too much for the Federal soldiers. Lieutenant Colonel William Chapman, commanding a brigade of U.S. Regulars near the left of the line, wrote that they "soon retired, exclaiming, 'It is too hot,' thus leaving our flank exposed."

Born in Prussia, John Koltes came to the United States at age 17 and was a substitute teacher at a Catholic school in Pittsburgh when the Mexican-American War broke out. After serving in the military during the conflict, he then served with the Marines at the U.S. mint in Philadelphia. When the Civil War began in 1861 he helped raise the 73rd Pennsylvania Infantry. A colonel at Second Manassas, he was killed by a Confederate shell atop Chinn Ridge. (loc)

Two more Confederate brigades, those under Brig. Gens. Lewis A. Armistead and Thomas F. Drayton, also arrived on the Union left. Despite General McDowell piecemealing another brigade of U.S. Regulars to plug gaps along the Sudley Road line, the dominoes began to fall. The weight of Mahone, Armistead, Drayton, and a section of the Washington Artillery sent the 83rd New York holding the left of the line out of the road and toward the crest of Henry Hill. With the left of Colonel Chapman's brigade now exposed, it too retired from the field. Further to the right, General Milroy's brigade gave way. The desperate Regulars spread out along the line commanded by Lt. Col. Robert Buchanan, with units retreating off their right and left, had no choice but to fall back toward the remnants of the Henry House.

The last of the Federal reserves, Col. Edward Ferrero's brigade from the IX Corps, went into a semi-circular position on the top of Henry Hill. It was Pope's last line of defense to allow his army to retreat unmolested back toward Centreville. A timid final push in the inky darkness by Confederates on Longstreet's far right was quickly ended by the men under Ferrero's watchful eye.

By 7 p.m. on the evening of August 30, Longstreet's massive attack against the left of Pope's position was over. No further movements were made against Henry

Hill, a reality largely due to the fact that Longstreet had utilized the entirety of his wing and had already committed his final reserves, units that arrived to the Sudley Road fight just as other actions across the battlefield died out. There were no more fresh soldiers among Longstreet's command to carry on the attack. Additionally, daylight was in short supply. A small cavalry action near the Portici plantation closed out the fighting that night.

Pope worked quickly now to save his army. At 6 p.m., he sent orders to VI Corps commander Maj. Gen. William B. Franklin back in Centreville to "post your command and whatever other troops you can collect and put them in the fortifications and other strong positions around Centreville, and hold those positions to the last extremity." Thirty minutes later, at 6:30 p.m., as the final shots of the battle rang out, Pope sent orders to Maj. Gen. Nathaniel P. Banks to "Destroy the public property at Bristoe [Station] and fall back upon Centreville at once."

Pope not only worked to secure his line of retreat, but also to establish a strong Federal presence in and around Centreville to deter Lee's pursuit any farther beyond that point. He needed to ensure Lee could get no closer to Washington. As the retreat was fully underway, Pope ordered Sigel's corps to move to the eastern bank of Young's Branch in order to cover the retreat of the rest of the army. Within just several hours, Sigel was then ordered to withdraw from that position and make for Centreville as well.

With Pope's army in full flight toward the stout defenses of Centreville, and the Confederate pursuit all but ended in the darkness of August 30, Lee sat down to write a dispatch to President Davis. From Groveton, at 10 p.m., Lee wrote that his army had "achieved on the plains of Manassas a signal victory over combined forces of Genls. McClellan and Pope." "We mourn the loss of our gallant dead in every conflict yet our gratitude to Almighty God for his mercies rises higher and higher each day, to Him and to the valour [sic] of our troops a nation's gratitude is due," Lee closed.

Despite Longstreet's inability to completely remove Pope's army from the chessboard of war in the Eastern theater that evening, he, like Lee, was extremely proud of his men's battlefield prowess. "The name of every officer, non-commissioned officer, and private who has shared in the toils and privations of this campaign should be mentioned," Longstreet closed his campaign report.

> *In one month these troops had marched over 200 miles upon little more than half rations and fought nine battles and skirmishes; killed, wounded, and captured nearly as many men as we had in our ranks, besides taking arms and other munitions of war in large quantities. I would that I could do justice to all of these gallant officers and men in this report.*

Lee had indeed achieved a great victory, but would he be able to continue to apply pressure on the Federal armies in their weakened state? Could he get at the "miscreant" Pope one more time before he reached the safety of the Washington defenses?

As Long as a Man Will Stand Up to the Work

CHAPTER ELEVEN

AUGUST 31–SEPTEMBER 1, 1862

Mother Nature added to the pall of the Federal reverses on the Second Manassas battlefield. Rain commenced falling from the skies on the evening of August 30, further dampening the spirits of the defeated Federals.

Yet for the disagreeable weather and the odious defeat, Pope's situation was not impossible. As darkness settled over the battlefield, the Confederate attack stalled, buying Pope several nighttime hours to prepare for whatever the next day might bring. Though Bull Run and its steep banks stood between Pope's men and the safety of Centreville's defenses four miles to the east, the final Union line had each flank strongly anchored on the stream. Pope pondered remaining in this position, but quickly dismissed it. He reported, "The very heavy losses we had suffered, and the complete prostration of our troops from hunger and fatigue, made it plain to me that we were no longer able, in the face of such overwhelming odds, to maintain our position so far to the front." At 8 p.m., Pope ordered his army back to Centreville. Watching the army retreat, Maj. Gen. Philip Kearny exclaimed, "It's another Bull Run, sir, it's another Bull Run!"

Throughout the night, soldiers clad in blue and caked in battle smoke, sweat, dust, and mud trudged along the Warrenton Turnpike to Centreville. One Yankee cavalryman protecting the army's rear wrote that the retreat was "such a sight I hope never to see again. Our men did not run, but regiments were

These two granite monuments, dedicated to fallen Union generals Phil Kearny and Isaac Stevens, were dedicated on the Ox Hill battlefield in October 1915. Among those in attendance at the dedication ceremony was a son of each of the generals, as well as some of their grandchildren and even great-grandchildren. (dw)

scattered like the leaves of autumn and all semblance of military organization lost. I think however that about <u>half</u> of our forces retired in <u>good order</u>."

Pope arrived in Centreville that night at the head of his army. He took time to inform General-in-Chief Halleck that "everything will go well" before turning to ensure that his optimistic prophecy became true. "Guide boards pointing out the location of the various corps, divisions and brigades" went up around Centreville and its defenses to sort out the confused mass that marched in from the west. From the other direction, soldiers of the Army of the Potomac's II and VI Corps filed to the front. They let the men under Pope have it by slinging insults in the direction of their failed general and his grandiose plans gone wrong.

The army commander spent August 31 not only resuscitating his army but also trying to rejuvenate his gloomy spirit. The shock of the previous day's defeat still hung over him when he told Halleck that his men would fight—before then painting a worse picture. "I should like to know whether you feel secure about Washington should this army be destroyed," Pope wrote. "I shall fight as long as a man will stand up to the work." Then, having already lost the initiative to Lee, Pope left his army's next move in Halleck's hands. "You must judge what is to be done, having in view the safety of the capital."

Robert E. Lee awoke on August 31 trying to hold the initiative and determine how to use it to his advantage against Pope. Centreville's defenses precluded a direct assault against the combined forces of Pope and McClellan. A quick look at a map revealed that the theater of operations had been whittled down to a large triangle of 40 square miles.

The western side of the triangle ran north from the Stone House intersection to the intersection of the Little River Turnpike and Gum Spring Road. The turnpike running northwest to southeast formed the triangle's second side and stretched 13 miles from the turnpike's intersection with Gum Spring Road to Germantown, a small crossroads town six miles east of Centreville where the Warrenton Turnpike collided with the Little River Turnpike. The triangle's southern base was Pope's most direct route back to Washington: the Warrenton Turnpike. Several roads ran roughly north-south from the southern side of the triangle to the Little River Turnpike.

In this triangular theater, Lee saw more opportunity that incurred little risk to his own army. Taking a maneuver from his toolbox that he had already utilized multiple times in this campaign, Lee ordered his army in motion once more around Pope's right flank. The task again fell to Jackson, who received orders to march along the Warrenton Turnpike in the direction of Germantown and Fairfax Court House beyond. Longstreet once again marched in Jackson's footsteps.

Lee's latest turning movement might catch Pope off guard and could lead to Confederate troops interposing themselves between the Federals and their capital. If Pope reacted, Lee's army could simply pull back, abandon the operation, and march north toward the Potomac River.

Jackson's column began marching shortly after noon on August 31. Tired from the previous week of marching and fighting, they only tramped ten miles before bedding down for the night, but slept on the right flank of Pope's Centreville position.

As Jackson's Confederates marched, they heard the distant sounds of cannon fire. Two brigades of cavalry under J. E. B. Stuart preceded the infantry. On their way to Germantown, Stuart's horsemen brushed aside two Federal cavalry patrols before engaging a stouter line of Union infantry and artillery near Germantown.

A sketch, titled "Union Defeat at Stone Bridge," shows both the destruction and retreat of Pope's army from the plains of Manassas. Completed in 1885, the drawing appears in the eponymous *Battles and Leaders* series. (b&l)

Pope handled this information while reviving his army. He talked boldly to Halleck of attacking the enemy in his front but did nothing to implement his idea. Then, understanding the Confederate intention of turning his flank and severing his route to Washington, Pope dispatched orders to one brigade "to open the road between this point and Fairfax Court-House, where the enemy has made his appearance."

Detailed instructions from Halleck made their way to Pope on the morning of September 1. Despite Pope's belief that the army should withdraw to Washington, Halleck told him not to do so yet. Instead, if Pope found the enemy trying to turn his position, Halleck instructed Pope to attack that column. If that attack was unsuccessful, Halleck said, "I suggest a gradual drawing in of your army to Fairfax Court-House, Annandale, or, if necessary . . . Alexandria." Staff officers raced from Pope's headquarters to set the army in motion to strike the enemy.

The first task at hand for Pope was to strengthen the Union line at Germantown to prevent Confederate seizure of the critical crossroads. To buy time for this line to be reinforced, Pope ordered Brig. Gen. Isaac Stevens to take two IX Corps divisions north using the Ox Road and establish a line in front of Germantown along the Little River Turnpike.

For once, luck smiled on the Federal army in this campaign. Jackson's column marched early that morning, but they did not march far. He stopped his men four miles short of Germantown, which Stuart reported was held by a strong enemy force. Jackson decided to wait for Longstreet's column to reinforce him before engaging. When Longstreet's column was in supporting distance of Jackson, "Stonewall" put his men back on the road. Two miles shy of their objective, they paused again atop Ox Hill.

Backed up by infantry, Stuart ordered his horse artillerists to the front. They blasted the Federal line at Germantown, but received worse than they handed out. Major General Joseph Hooker was in command of a growing force there. Jackson and Stuart did not believe the line could be broken without a large attack. Lee's orders to fight only if circumstances favored his army echoed in the back of Stuart's and Jackson's minds; Jackson decided to wait for the army commander to reach the front and decide for himself what the next step would be.

While Jackson could not break the Germantown line, he did not think the Federals there would advance and attack him. He did learn of a Federal advance from the south (Stevens' two divisions) and sent skirmishers south from the Little River Turnpike to screen his column.

Stevens's off-road march brought his military column onto a small cart path meant for moving cattle and farm wagons, not soldiers and artillery. After two miles of this march, Stevens's column emerged into an open field. There, in front of them, just 200 yards away, Stevens saw Jackson's skirmishers. The Union general ordered his own skirmishers forward and deployed the rest of his infantry and artillery behind this screen. The Federal skirmishers quickly won the upper hand and drove their Confederate counterparts back. As they did so, they revealed Jackson's main position at Ox Hill.

Isaac Stevens now realized his objective of seizing a defensive position along the Little River Turnpike was impossible with Jackson's large force in front of him. Attempting to seize whatever initiative he had, Stevens decided to attack to spoil whatever Jackson's plans might have been.

The ground over which Stevens decided to attack was four sided, surrounded by woods on its east, north, and west sides. The same unfinished railroad that aided Jackson's men at Second Manassas formed the south end of the field. Jackson's line was in the woods on the north side of the open field and on both sides of the Ox Road.

Stevens was not aware of the odds against him, but he knew his force was not large. His own division numbered 2,000 men while Reno's supporting division was hardly larger, weighing in at 2,400 strong. Stevens deployed his own division into three lines, spearheaded by Stevens's 79th New York Highlanders, his original command. Stevens dispatched one of Reno's brigades into the woods east of Ox Road to protect his flank as he attacked and brought more artillery to the front to add more punch to his assault. Lastly, he spurred one of his staff officers back to the Warrenton Turnpike to call on Pope for help.

Jackson finished deploying his command for the meeting engagement. Starke's division held the wooded ground east of Ox Road. Lawton's division bulged back from the main line and held the center while

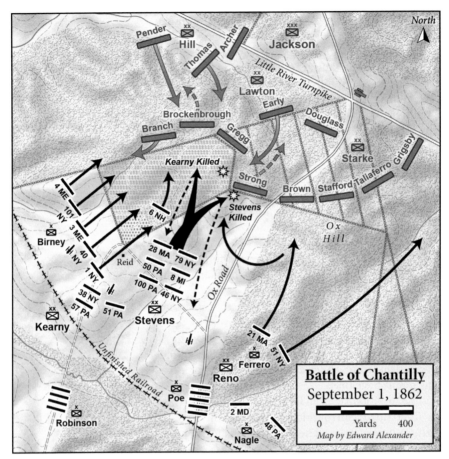

BATTLE OF CHANTILLY—Following the Federal withdrawal to Centreville, Robert E. Lee sent "Stonewall" Jackson on another turning movement around Pope's army. This resulted in the battle of Chantilly, a battle that resulted in more casualties (including the deaths of two Union generals) and the end of the Second Manassas campaign.

A. P. Hill's Confederates anchored the Confederate right. He had 17,000 men to fight the coming battle.

At 4:30 p.m., Stevens's line surged uphill into the face of heavy enemy fire. The Federal general personally led his men forward on foot. Distant lightning added a haunting rumbling to the growing sound of battle. Once the Union line came within range of Jackson's men, the Confederates opened a staggering fire that blunted the Yankees. Stevens tried to rally his men and urged them forward to within 75 yards of Jackson's line, but no closer. Five of the Highlanders' color bearers went down. At this moment, Stevens grabbed the flag of the Highlanders from a begrudgingly stubborn color bearer who only gave up his duty at Stevens's urging.

"We are all Highlanders," Stevens yelled. "Follow Highlanders; forward my Highlanders!" Stevens led the 79th New York and 28th Massachusetts straight into the teeth of Lawton's division. There, confusion reigned in the Southern ranks. They broke under the renewed pressure. Stevens and his men charged into the woods bordering the northern end of the open field. As soon as Stevens personally crossed the fence separating the field from the woods, a bullet hit him in the temple. He was dead before he hit the ground, falling with the flag of the Highlanders still in his lifeless grasp.

Now the heavens opened, bringing heavy winds, thunder and lightning, and a driving rain. It was "one of the wildest rainstorms I ever witnessed," recalled one Confederate who survived the battle and the storm. Three regiments of Brig. Gen. Jubal Early's brigade arrived with the weather to plug the gap in Lawton's line. Stevens's death, the waning momentum of an offensive assault, and Early's counterattack drove Stevens's attack back on both sides of Ox Road. By 5:30 p.m., only the sound of artillery, skirmish fire, and nature's thunder roared around Ox Hill as the battle slowed.

While Stevens and his men fought for their lives, the staff officer Stevens sent to the rear to find help encountered the one-armed, fiery General Phil Kearny. When told of Stevens's call for aid, Kearny responded, "By God, I will support Stevens anywhere!" Kearny led Brig. Gen. David Birney's brigade forward to the sound of Stevens's fight.

Upon arriving at the scene of the fighting, Birney found the sickly Reno, who ordered Birney's men into the cornfield fronting the Confederate position. Birney's men quickly engaged Hill's division. Having been in the fight longer, Hill worried about his dampened ammunition; he sent a courier to Jackson asking for help. Jackson replied to the courier, "Give my compliments to General Hill, and tell him that the Yankee ammunition is as wet as his; to stay where he is." Hill could not withdraw.

Birney could not drive back the enemy in his front, either. He, too, worried because the troops that Kearny ordered to support his right had not arrived. Kearny personally tried to rally and lead Stevens's men into the vacant position, but they refused to budge. Kearny continued riding to find help and located the 21st Massachusetts east of Ox Road. He quickly ordered them to Birney's right. They did so cautiously in the smoke-covered, rain-soaked, darkening battlefield.

Sensing their hesitation and seeing no reason for it, Kearny tried to urge the Bay Staters forward. They presented some recently captured prisoners to support their case that a large body of the enemy was nearby. "God damn you and your prisoners!" scowled Kearny. He twisted the reins of his horse and turned it in the direction of where the Massachusetts man believed the enemy to be.

Twenty yards from where he scolded the 21st Massachusetts, Kearny stumbled upon more soldiers. "What troops are these?" A voice shouted back, "The 49th Georgia." Kearny calmly said, "All right," and wheeled his horse back to friendly lines. The Georgians knew this was a Yankee officer, put their guns to their shoulders, and squeezed off a scattered volley. One bullet found its mark, striking Kearny in the rear end and passing through his torso. Kearny toppled from his horse, dead before he hit the soaked earth.

The Georgians charged forward before being stopped by the 21st Massachusetts. Birney, now in charge, tried to bring more men to the field, though they were not utilized. Birney recognized the futility of trying to break the enemy lines.

Attempting to perform a reconnaissance himself, Maj. Gen. Kearny was vigorous and conspicuous on the field on September 1. He fumbled into Confederate lines and was killed while trying to escape the hail of bullets. Gen. Lee had his body and possessions sent back through the lines following the battle. (loc)

Originally buried at Trinity Church in New York, Phil Kearny was reinterred in Arlington National Cemetery in 1911 and then moved in 1914 to his present location beneath a memorial statue. Edward Clark Potter—the man who sculpted the marble lions in front of the New York Public Library—created the sculpture, which, according to Arlington National Cemetery, sits in "an artistic setting that [harmonizes] with the size and dignity of the Monument." (cm)

Both sides mutually called off the fight. Longstreet arrived within supporting distance of Jackson. The tired Confederates under Jackson watched as the Federals in their front withdrew. By 3 a.m. the next morning, the last Federals left the field. Behind them lay the casualties of the closing action of the Second Manassas campaign at Chantilly and Ox Hill: 500 Confederates and 700 Federals.

By the time Stevens attacked Jackson at Ox Hill, Jackson and Stuart had already called off assaulting Hooker's Germantown line, thus preserving the Federal route to Washington. Lee would allow Pope's battered army to get there safely. The defenses of the Federal capital were too strong. Lee could not hurt Pope any more.

Never Such a Campaign

E P I L O G U E

The hard hand of war had returned once again to Manassas. Just thirteen months after the battle of First Manassas on the plains thereof, two larger, veteran armies engaged there once more. As the Federal army retreated on the evening of August 30, Confederate soldiers walking over the field saw a slaughter they had not yet seen during the war.

After midnight on August 30, a soldier in the 1st Georgia Infantry noted that "a slow drizzly rain" only added to the misery and gloom of the battle's aftermath. This same soldier also saw a farm house that was converted into an ad hoc field hospital. "The groans of the wounded and dying was awful to listen to," he wrote. "Arms and legs were piled in heaps, while numbers of those who had their limbs amputated were lying around in the house and yard, dead."

Men in the 7th North Carolina Infantry were ordered to the rear on August 31 to draw supplies. Unlike the scenes that played out at the field hospitals, these Tar Heels witnessed the state of the dead in rapid decomposition. One soldier in the unit wrote, "The sight was truly appalling." He saw "dead men and horses in a state of putrefaction" everywhere, while "The stench was well nigh intolerable." Sergeant Draughton S. Haynes, 49th Georgia, noted, "Many of the Yankees bodies had turned perfectly black, and to pass them would almost make a person vomit."

At another location on the battlefield, Georgian W. H. Andrews saw where the ground around a Federal

Private James Jerman Palmer, Co. K, Palmetto South Carolina Sharpshooters, was killed in action on August 30, 1862, at the age of 22. His older brother was killed two years later in battle near Atlanta. Today, James's remains rest in Groveton Confederate Cemetery, a part of Manassas National Battlefield Park. (dw)

Also buried in Groveton Confederate Cemetery is William Goodwyn Ridley. Great grandson of Revolutionary War colonel Thomas Ridley, William enlisted at age 19 in July 1861 with the 6th Virginia Infantry. He died of a head wound just 13 months later on August 30, 1862. (dw)

battery caught fire during the battle. It consumed the bodies of dead Federal soldiers where the fire raged. These were "Horrible sights to look upon with their clothing burnt off and their flesh to a blackened crisp." In still other areas of the battlefield, Andrews witnessed some who had died still "on their knees . . . grasping their guns, others died eating, with their hands and mouths full of crackers." The sickening sight led Andrews to think he "could never eat another cracker" again.

The Federal retreat on August 31 did not shield that army from witnessing some of the horrific scenes that the devastation of the battle produced. Private Charles H. Veil, a soldier in the 9th Pennsylvania Reserves, remembered one of these scenes as his regiment passed through Centreville during their retreat. It was "a sight I often think of," he wrote. Veil watched as "surgeons were operating on the badly wounded . . . cutting off arms, feet, hands and limbs of all kinds." The surgeon's work, done in what Veil described as "a little country school house," had amputated arms and legs "thrown out an open window." "The cut-off limbs had accumulated so that they blocked the window, and a detail of a few men were hauling away the limbs with a wheelbarrow," he continued. "It had the appearance of a human slaughter house," and "was an awful sight" that he never forgot during the years after the war.

Yet for many in both armies, a year of war had radically changed these men. With each battle, the sights and sounds of the dead and dying, and those fighting for their lives at field hospitals in their wake, had numbed their senses to the realities of war. It had also removed any romantic notions so many men had taken into the armies in the spring of 1861. Looking at the wounded, dead, and dying in front of him, William Andrews spoke for many of his comrades when he wrote, "We are getting pretty well hardened to such sights, and can look on a dead man with the same feelings we would a hog at home, in hog-killing time."

Although Lee achieved victories at Brawner Farm, Thoroughfare Gap, Manassas, and Chantilly, they came at an enormous cost. The Army of Northern Virginia sustained losses of 1,300 dead and 7,000 wounded. They were casualties Lee could ill afford, especially after the continual campaigns and engagements these units had participated in since May. Lee had already written Davis twice toward the end of the battle where, among other things, he pushed for reinforcements that simply were not coming to his army. Worse still, these high casualty numbers were the result of two days of fighting that had been fought defensively, while "the third had witnessed a rout of the enemy."

There were other takeaways for the Confederate army as a result of the Second Manassas campaign. Artillerist E. P. Alexander contended that it molded the fighting spirit of the men in the Army of Northern Virginia, in which they had "acquired that magnificent morale which made them equal to twice their numbers." The army that was molded in August 1862 under the command of Lee also came to represent the command structure it held until the death of "Stonewall" Jackson in May 1863.

The campaign also molded the army commander. This was the first campaign General Lee prosecuted by himself, from beginning to end. Here he demonstrated numerous attributes of leadership, strategic and tactical thinking, and the ability to read his opponents—aspects that defined his leadership of the Army of Northern Virginia and placed him among our country's finest generals. An article in the *Richmond Times Dispatch* from September 3, 1862, supported the argument contemporaneously when they wrote:

> *The Commander-in-Chief of the Confederate army has achieved new renown by the splendid combinations which have resulted in another crushing defeat of the Federalists. As modest and unpretending as the Yankee Generals are boastful and false, he quietly permits results to speak for him, and those results prove him one of the greatest military leaders of modern times. We congratulate the country that it has at the head of its armies this calm, self-poised, consummate soldier— one who both as General and gentleman is a worthy representative of the glorious South.*

Lee's maneuvering and successful battles in August 1862 opened all of central Virginia and most of the state's northern region. With victory animating the common soldiers and generals of the Army of Northern Virginia, Lee set his sights on Maryland and Pennsylvania north of the Potomac River.

Perhaps the greatest fruit of the Confederate victory, though, was the blow to morale in the Federal army and the will to keep fighting by the northern home front. One northerner wrote, "I feel ashamed of being an American now. . . . To think that we should be conquered by the bare feet and rags of the South." John W. Chase, an artillerist in the 1st Massachusetts Light Artillery, wrote his brother from the safety of Alexandria, Virginia on September 3, that he had "nothing to say about the recent battles for I am ashamed to hear anything about them for I think it was a disgrace to us as a nation and begin to think it is about time to stop talking about Conquering the South when we cannot get possession of one state."

Not only did the rank and file feel the effects of their defeat at Manassas, so too did many officers. Major General John Sedgwick, a division commander in the Army of the Potomac's II Corps, was so dispirited by the defeat and potential future that he confided in a letter to his sister on September 4, "I look to division as certain; the only question is where the line is to run." Brigade commander Col. Orlando Poe, also of the Army of the Potomac, concurred with Sedgwick that the defeat at Second Manassas marked the beginning of the end of the war. "I believe that the war is nearly over . . . [and] I am more despondent than ever before."

The impact of yet another military defeat in the Eastern Theater stretched further than just deflated morale. The destruction and rout of the Army of Virginia and elements of the Army of Potomac cost several officers devastating blows to their careers. General Irvin McDowell's numerous mistakes during the month of August led to his career being sidelined for the next two years. No new assignments came until July 1864 when he was shipped out to California to command the Department of the Pacific. General Fitz John Porter's army career was not just sidelined, it was over. Army commander Pope leveled charges of "willful failure to obey his orders" during the battle on August 29. Porter faced a court-martial, and was found guilty of misconduct and disobedience on January 10, 1863. Eleven days later he was cashiered from the army. It took 23 years before his actions that day were found to be justified and his commission in the army restored.

There were other officers that held various levels of culpability for the defeat at Second Manassas, as well. Recently appointed General-in-Chief Henry W. Halleck came into his position against chaos and confusion, both politically and militarily. It was perhaps his toughest, but necessary, decision to order George McClellan and the Army of the Potomac off the Peninsula that contributed to the army's defeat. Halleck's order surrendered the strategic initiative in Virginia to Robert E. Lee. As campaign after campaign, battle after battle proved as the war progressed, Lee became a master of the field when he commanded the initiative.

Coupled with Halleck's decision was the time it took to unite both armies. "Little Mac's" withdrawal from Harrison's Landing gave Lee and his army more time to breathe and operate against Pope without both armies fully uniting. Abraham Lincoln believed that McClellan had "acted badly" in his role in Pope's ultimate defeat.

Major General John Pope held the lion's share of responsibility for the defeat at Manassas. John Chase wrote his brother on September 1, "I reckon the people of this great country will find out that Gen Pope is not a great sight bigger Gen than McClellan." Yet, two days later, in another letter to his brother, Chase gave the defeated and disgraced Kentucky general grace. "Pope I have no doubt he is a good Gen but think he advertised rather large on the start," Chase wrote, "and I guess he has found out that Richmond is not so easily taken." He continued, "I will not find fault for I feel as though every one should try and put there [sic] Shoulder to the wheel once more and see if we ever are going to do anything."

Many more, however, took Pope to task contemporaneously, as have historians over the last 160-plus years. Few have been able to look past the defeat of August 30 to examine the campaign as a whole. After all, until August 30, Pope had bested Lee on almost every occasion.

Despite the treatment of Pope in the historiography, he was not banished to the West, nor did he sit idly for a command after his defeat. Clearly both Lincoln and Stanton saw something useful in the general and trusted him despite his defeat at Second Manassas. First sent to the Department of the Northwest in Minnesota, he oversaw the Federal effort in the Dakota War. By March 1865, he commanded the Military Division of Missouri and the Department of Arkansas, which numbered 41,000 troops and geographically stretched over half the size of the United States.

In the end, however, the defeat at Second Manassas lay with Pope. His failures were numerous, from the strategic down to the tactical. Although he understood the many deficiencies of his army before he even took command, he failed to take them into account when he planned. His time schedules for troop movements went beyond feasible. He failed to trust his subordinates, struggled to accept accurate intelligence, and, by late morning on August 30, had lost his sense of reality related to the tactical situation on the field. Pope never fully grasped the role of the cavalry for his army and the campaign, and thus did not use it to his advantage. Additionally, Pope could not see beyond bagging Jackson, his whole strategy boiling down to that singular mission.

Perhaps the final analysis of the Second Manassas campaign was best summed up by William Dorsey Pender. A brigadier general in Jackson's wing during the campaign, Pender reflected, "There never was such a campaign, not even by Napoleon."

William Dorsey Pender's humble beginnings changed upon his appointment to West Point at the age of sixteen. Cutting his teeth in the army while stationed on the Pacific coast, upon his resignation in March 1861, he entered the Confederate army as a colonel and was promoted to brigadier general just two months before Second Manassas. (loc)

Union and Confederate Cavalry at Second Manassas

APPENDIX A

BY DANIEL T. DAVIS

The unrelenting heat of August 1862 did not deter Gen. Robert E. Lee and Maj. Gen. John Pope as their armies faced one another in central Virginia. Following the battle of Cedar Mountain, both commands prepared to resume operations and their respective cavalry forces stood poised to play a supporting, but critical, role in the coming weeks.

Lee met with his key subordinates at Orange Court House on August 17. The Confederate commander planned to pry Pope from his position along the Rapidan River. Lee instructed the head of his cavalry division, Maj. Gen. James Ewell Brown "Jeb" Stuart, to push his command over Raccoon Ford and cut communications in Pope's rear at Culpeper while the infantry assailed Pope's front.

In preparation for this movement, Stuart planned to rendezvous with one of his brigades under Brig. Gen. Fitzhugh Lee at Verdiersville, a nearby cluster of buildings along the Orange Plank Road. Lee, however, delayed his march to join Stuart to allow his men to collect rations. Stuart, along with members of his staff, bedded down for the night, unbeknownst of Lee's decision. Later in the evening, at the sound of approaching horses, Stuart's adjutant, Maj. Norman Fitzhugh, left the bivouac to investigate.

The horsemen turned out to be detachments of the 1st Michigan and 5th New York Cavalry under Col. Thornton Brodhead from Brig. Gen. John Buford's brigade. Brodhead's troopers were returning from a reconnaissance to Louisa Court House when the head of the column captured Fitzhugh. Thundering into Stuart's camp, the Union cavalry scattered the Confederates. Brodhead's foray bagged not only Stuart's famous plumed hat but papers outlining Lee's intention to attack Pope. This intelligence soon made its way to Union headquarters and Pope immediately began planning a march from the Rapidan for a new position on the north bank of the Rappahannock. River.

Portici, the Lewis family home, stood atop the hill in the distance. It witnessed the largest cavalry engagement of the Civil War up to that time on August 30, 1862 during the closing stages of the battle of Second Manassas. (kp)

New Hampshire native Thornton F. Brodhead was a Harvard graduate, state senator from Michigan, Mexican-American War veteran, and postmaster for Detroit before the Civil War. He helped raise the 1st Michigan Infantry in the fall of 1861. Brodhead died of his wounds from the fighting at Second Manassas on August 31, 1862. (loc)

Pope detailed his cavalry under Buford and Brig. Gen. George Bayard to cover his withdrawal. Bayard spent August 18 guarding wagon trains before moving first to Culpeper and then to Brandy Station, a stop on the Orange and Alexandria Railroad. On the morning of August 20, Bayard dispatched scouting parties that encountered Stuart, riding at the advance of Lee's pursuing infantry. Bayard decided to fight a delaying action as he pulled back to the Rappahannock.

"As the rebels . . . rushed madly down . . . a stunning discharge tore through the charging squadrons," a soldier in the 1st New Jersey recalled. "The cloud of dust eddied as if in the circles of a whirlwind, while from its envelopment rose up a frightful chorus of shrieks and groans . . . twice more did the breech-loading carbines pour in their fatal fire. Then from the midst of the dust and smoke, a few staggering men and horses broke away to the rear, leaving most of the charging party bleeding upon the ground." Despite the brief and brutal fight, Bayard managed to extricate his brigade and reached the safety of the river and the rest of Pope's army.

Bayard and Buford continued to picket the Rappahannock over the next few days. Their efforts proved fruitful but frustrating to Robert E. Lee. Once again, a river separated Lee from his foe. "Our positions on the south bank of the Rappahannock were commanded by those of the enemy, who guarded all the fords, it was determined to seek a more favorable place to cross higher up on the river," he wrote. Lee shifted his infantry to the vicinity of Beverly's Ford and the Hazel River, a tributary of the Rappahannock. Lee directed Maj. Gen. Thomas J. "Stonewall" Jackson and elements from his wing to cross the Hazel at Welford's Ford and move along the Rappahannock. Jackson's incursion allowed Stuart an opportunity to slice into Pope's rear. Stuart charged into Catlett's Station on the night of August 22, capturing stores and prisoners. He also brought back information that Maj. Gen. George B. McClellan's Army of the Potomac was en route from the Virginia Peninsula to reinforce Pope. This news motivated Lee to strike before the two forces could converge. Lee decided to detach Jackson on a flanking movement beyond Pope's right to cut the Orange and Alexandria Railroad, Pope's main supply line.

Jackson initiated his march on the morning of August 25. He passed through Salem, then headed through the Bull Run Mountains toward Gainesville. There, Jackson met Stuart with the bulk of Fitz Lee's brigade along with that of Brig. Gen. Beverly Robertson. Jackson then detached his advance guard, Col. Thomas Munford's 2nd Virginia Cavalry, toward Bristoe Station. Munford "approached within one hundred yards before the enemy was aware of his presence, dispersed a cavalry company, which constituted a part of the guard, and captured forty-three infantry," wrote a member of Stuart's staff. With this station firmly in hand, the Confederates moved on to capture Pope's main depot at Manassas Junction.

The destruction of his supplies prompted Pope to abandon the Rappahannock and set out to find Jackson. Bayard again drew the assignment of screening the blue infantry. His brigade marched from Warrenton on August 26 and accompanied Maj. Gen. Franz Sigel's I Corps to Gainesville. The same day, Lee, with Maj. Gen. James Longstreet's wing, pushed over the Rappahannock in an effort to find Jackson and reunite his command.

From Gainesville, elements of Bayard's brigade moved to occupy Thoroughfare Gap. "Trees had been felled all along from one height to the other, and immense rocks rolled down the hill-side among them," wrote a trooper in the 1st New Jersey. "Earth was cast lighting upon the branches, and ravines converted into traps for the unwary; until no horse could expect to pass with life, and even infantry would be obliged to carefully pick their way."

Lead elements of Longstreet's wing soon arrived. "A small party of infantry was sent into the mountain to reconnoiter," Longstreet wrote. "Passing through the Gap, Colonel Benjamin Beck, of the Ninth Georgia Regiment, met the enemy, but was obliged to retire." Running up against stiff resistance from the Union cavalry, Longstreet pushed more men into the fight. The dismounted horsemen soon gave way to Brig. Gen. James Ricketts's infantry and brought Longstreet to a halt. Undeterred, Longstreet moved around the Union flank, forcing Ricketts to retreat.

Stuart, meanwhile, remained with Jackson. Following the destruction of the supplies at Manassas Junction, Jackson fell back to high ground overlooking the Warrenton Turnpike and assumed a position along an unfinished railroad cut near the hamlet of Groveton. On the morning of August 28, Stuart rode out to establish communications with Longstreet.

After graduating from West Point, like many other officers of the day, George Bayard served frontier duty in Colorado and Kansas. Appointed colonel of the 1st Pennsylvania Cavalry at the outbreak of the Civil War, by the spring of 1862 he was promoted to brigadier general of volunteers and placed in charge of the cavalry of the III Corps. (loc)

Brigadier General Beverly Robertson was dismissed from the U.S. Army on August 8, 1861 for "having given proof of his disloyalty." The claim was just; he had been appointed a captain, and later a colonel in the Confederate army five months prior yet continued to serve in the U.S. Army. (na)

The Confederate cavalrymen encountered Bayard's brigade at Haymarket and skirmished briefly in the afternoon. Both sides broke off the fight and Stuart returned to Jackson's wing to protect his right flank. That night, Jackson attacked Union infantry under Brig. Gen. Rufus King, out searching for the Confederates.

Jackson dispatched Stuart again the next morning. "Just after leaving the Sudley road, my party was fired on from the woods bordering the road," Stuart wrote. A sharp engagement ensued, and Stuart promptly brought up his horse artillery under Capt. John Pelham, whose deadly fire cleared the way for Stuart to continue his mission. With Jackson and Pope's guns rumbling in the distance, Stuart "met with the head of General Longstreet's column between Haymarket and Gainesville, and there communicated to the commanding general General Jackson's position and the enemy's."

Longstreet began moving up to link in with Jackson's line. Stuart continued to screen this movement and deployed his available cavalry along a ridge near Longstreet's right flank. From there, Stuart observed Union infantry in the distance. He smartly sent word back of the Federal presence and ordered his men to drag branches along the ground to create dust and the illusion of a strong force. Confederate infantry soon arrived and secured Stuart's sector.

On the morning of August 30, Stuart awoke to find "the enemy had materially retired his left wing." He galloped forward to assess the situation and found Pope massed for an assault on Jackson's line. Around the middle of the afternoon, Longstreet's infantry launched their own attack. As the gray infantry got under way, Stuart, with Robertson and Col. Thomas Rosser's 5th Virginia Cavalry, went forward on the Confederate right. "The Lord of Hosts was plainly fighting on our side, and the solid walls of Federal infantry melted away before the straggling, but nevertheless determined onsets of our infantry columns," Stuart proudly wrote. Longstreet's attack completely smashed the Union lines and blue infantry retreated eastward toward Bull Run.

Advancing up a ridge occupied by the Lewis House, Robertson encountered Munford's 2nd Virginia along with Union cavalry. A squadron from the 2nd advanced and scattered the blue cavalry, only to find regiments from Buford's brigade positioned

Just two weeks before graduating from West Point, Thomas Rosser resigned from the institution to join the Confederate cause in April 1861. His Confederate army service included time with the Washington Artillery of New Orleans before being appointed colonel of the 5th Virginia Cavalry. (loc)

behind them. "When . . . our regiment came to [the] top of [a] hill on our right, the enemy were drawn up in line of battle on the opposite hill about 400 yards distant," remembered Capt. Samuel Myers of the 7th Virginia Cavalry. Buford deployed the 1st Michigan Cavalry, 4th New York Cavalry, and 1st West Virginia Cavalry in an effort to stem the Confederate advance.

"I ordered [my] regiment to charge with drawn sabers on their right flank," wrote Captain Myers. "The whole command obeyed with the greatest alacrity, charging upon them with shouts that made the very welkin ring." Colonel Asher Harman's 12th Virginia Cavalry also joined in the attack. Harman recalled the Confederate cavalry pushed Buford back "in complete disorder." "I pursued them over the run and as far as the pike near the stone bridge," he recalled. Buford received a wound during this sharp action while Colonel Brodhead fell mortally wounded.

Pope's battered army streamed toward Washington, leaving Lee the victor on the battlefield. The engagements at Brandy Station, Thoroughfare Gap, Haymarket, and along the banks of Bull Run seasoned the mounted arms of both armies. It was, however, a prelude to the days to come when troopers in blue and gray would clash on bloody fields in Virginia, Maryland, and Pennsylvania.

DANIEL T. DAVIS *is a senior education associate at the American Battlefield Trust. He is a founding contributor with* Emerging Civil War *and co-author of six books in Savas Beatie's Emerging Civil War Series. He has also authored or co-authored articles in* Blue & Gray Magazine *and* Civil War Times.

T 49
FORT BUFFALO

Nearby once stood Fort Buffalo. This earthwork fortification was built by the 21st New York Infantry of the Union army in 1861 and named for the troops' hometown. During the Civil War, a concentration of forts existed in the Seven Corners section of Falls Church. These structures were used in the Federal defense of Washington. First occupied by Brig. Gen. Irvin McDowell's troops during the First Manassas Campaign, the fort was briefly occupied by the Confederates following that Federal defeat in July 1861. In the 1950s, Seven Corners shopping center and the surrounding community was developed on land once part of and surrounding Fort Buffalo.

DEPARTMENT OF HISTORIC RESOURCES, 1995

Miscommunication and Mistrust: Federal High Command at Second Manassas

APPENDIX B

BY KEVIN R. PAWLAK

For 134 days in the spring and summer of 1862, the Union war effort in Virginia was run from the offices of the Executive Mansion and War Department rather than from the field. During that time, the success of Federal armies resembled a bell curve—rising in the spring of 1862 with victories in Tennessee, peaking with the Army of the Potomac within a half dozen miles of Richmond, and descending as Federal advances across the country stalled. In the midst of their joint command tenure, President Abraham Lincoln and Secretary of War Edwin Stanton made decisions that fostered an environment in which their generals "found that criticizing other generals and injecting friction and mistrust into the chain of command brought rewards rather than punishment," according to author Ethan Rafuse.

Worse yet, upon his assumption of command of the Army of Virginia on June 26, 1862, Maj. Gen. John Pope, newly arrived from the west, did not see eye to eye with the Army of the Potomac's commander, Maj. Gen. George B. McClellan. The same could be said of McClellan's views toward Pope.

The two men were certainly aware of one another prior to the Civil War. Early in that conflict, McClellan and Pope corresponded as superior to subordinate. But Pope's coming east was different, and it dramatically altered their relationship. President Abraham Lincoln and Secretary of War Edwin Stanton expected both men to work together to achieve final victory in Virginia. The first correspondence between them would have brightened Lincoln's and Stanton's hope that this would work.

"I beg you to understand that it is my earnest wish to cooperate in the heartiest and most energetic manner with you," Pope said on July 4. McClellan reciprocated three days later, approving of Pope's plans and promising "to be in daily communication with you both by telegraph and by letter."

Privately, though, Pope and McClellan expressed misgivings about the other. Behind closed doors, Pope

The famous encounter between Pope and McClellan occurred near the site of Fort Buffalo. There is nothing left of the fort today. (dw)

A wartime image of the northwest facade of the White House, also known as the Executive Mansion. It was from here that Stanton and Lincoln tried unsuccessfully to run the war effort in the spring and early summer of 1862. This image was taken and reproduced by Bell & Brother. (loc)

expressed "a bitter hatred" of McClellan to his subordinates. To Lincoln's cabinet, Pope openly stated his "distrust" of McClellan and pushed for McClellan's removal from command. He reiterated that he expected no help from McClellan.

McClellan's first private jab at Pope came on July 22 after the release of Pope's addresses and orders to the Army of Virginia, which took shots at the Army of the Potomac (whether that was Pope's intention or not). "I see that the Pope bubble is likely to be suddenly collapsed," he declared.

Into all of this—at Pope's suggestion—came Maj. Gen. Henry W. Halleck to assume the role of General-in-Chief. Halleck's appointment became official on July 23, 1862, 134 days after McClellan had been relieved of that duty on March 11, 1862. Immediately upon arriving in Virginia, Halleck had to determine strategy between the two separated armies. Halleck had three options: bring the Army of the Potomac to the Army of Virginia in northern Virginia, combine the two armies on the Virginia Peninsula, or keep them apart. A proponent of concentration, Halleck dismissed the last option outright. To settle upon a decision, he visited McClellan and his army in its camps around Harrison's Landing, on the Peninsula 25 miles from Richmond.

Halleck recognized the awkward nature of this discussion, not least because the two differed regarding their plan. Halleck believed McClellan's army should leave the Peninsula to join Pope; McClellan believed he should receive reinforcements and resume operations against Richmond. "It certainly was unpleasant to tell one who had been my superior in rank that his plans were wrong," Halleck stated. About a week after his visit, Halleck ordered the Army of the Potomac off the Peninsula to join Pope's army. Once together, the combined forces would advance on Richmond from the north and crush the Confederates in front of them.

The Army of the Potomac's withdrawal down the Peninsula was, in the words of Halleck, "one of the most difficult things to achieve successfully that an accomplished commander could execute." Halleck ordered the movement on August 3, but preparing the army for this massive undertaking took time, and McClellan's men did not leave their camps until August 14 at the earliest. As Pope and McClellan— two rivals whose enmity towards one another was growing—prepared to merge their forces, questions arose that neither could find an answer to.

The biggest question in both generals' minds was who would command the combined armies. During his Harrsion's Landing visit, Halleck told McClellan that he would take charge of the combined force. Halleck reiterated that to McClellan on August 7. Pope believed "that as soon as the whole of our forces were concentrated," Halleck would "take command in person, and that when everything was ready we were to move forward in concert."

At the time when Halleck was needed most to orchestrate the concentration of the two armies as Lee's forces pressured Pope and further complicated the situation, Halleck began to crack under the weight of his new position. "I feel broken down every night with the heat, labor and responsibility, but am in good health," he wrote on August 9. He likewise found himself caught between McClellan and the Lincoln administration, whose patience with the general quickly waned.

When the lead elements of the Army of the Potomac began reaching the campaign's front lines along the Rappahannock River on August 20, Halleck could not provide enough information to either Pope or McClellan to effect the junction of their armies. From far away and over a month ago, Pope and McClellan had vowed to work with one another, even to stay in daily contact. Now, as they physically neared each other and Halleck in Washington, that communication broke down and detrimentally plagued Halleck's plan.

General Samuel Heintzelman and his staff had this image taken in early August 1862 while the Army of the Potomac encamped around Harrison's Landing on the Virginia Peninsula. Just weeks later, his III Corps was engaged at Second Manassas. (loc)

On August 24, McClellan inquired of Halleck, "Please inform me immediately exactly where Pope is & what [he is] doing . . . ." When Maj. Gen. Fitz John Porter's V Corps reached where they thought Pope's army was, they found Rappahannock Station devoid of soldiers with no word of where Pope had gone. "Please inform me exactly where General Pope's troops are," pleaded McClellan. A testy Halleck shot back, "You ask me for information which I cannot give. I do not know either where General Pope is or where the enemy in force is."

Confusion and a dearth of meaningful communication were not the only problems plaguing

Pope, McClellan, and Halleck regarding how and where the two armies were supposed to unite. Pope and McClellan pondered what the command situation would be when the Army of Virginia and the Army of the Potomac became one. McClellan was Pope's senior, but McClellan had clearly fallen out of favor with the Lincoln Administration while Pope had not.

As previously stated, Pope supposed Halleck would command the joint armies. But he was still unsure. "I am not acquainted with your views," wrote Pope on August 25, "as you seem to suppose, and would be glad to know them as far as my own position and operations are concerned."

McClellan equally expressed confusion about the command situation. The day before Pope stated his uncertainty to Halleck, McClellan asked the General-in-Chief "whether you still intend to place me in the command" of both armies. McClellan had reason to believe this to be the case. On August 7, Halleck told him, "it is my intention that you shall command all the troops in Virginia as soon as we can get them together." However, the rumor mill swirled around McClellan. He confided to his friend Burnside, "Yesterday and to-day I have received intelligence from confidential sources leading me to think it probable that Halleck either will not or cannot carry out his intentions in regard to my position, as expressed to you. This shall make no difference with me. I shall push on everything just as if I were to remain in command."

For two headstrong men clambering for promotion who disliked their rival, this confusion of command did not help bring about their cooperation.

Throughout the weeks-long process of combining the two armies, Halleck had stressed that the junction of both forces was to dictate all other decisions made. By August 29, when Pope gathered his army on the old Manassas battlefield to deal with "Stonewall" Jackson's forces, McClellan and Pope had nearly completed the junction for which Halleck had advocated for less than one month earlier. But bringing about the concentration of the two armies in the face of the enemy was easier said than done.

The easiest and least bloody way to do that would have been for Pope to disengage from Jackson (and

General Fitz John Porter could have little imagined that his army career would come to a crashing end just weeks following this image being struck on August 8, 1862. With his headquarters staff present, this image was also taken at Harrison's Landing along the James River before the Army of the Potomac left the Peninsula. (loc)

unknowingly Longstreet), bring his army east of Bull Run, and meet the remnants of the Army of the Potomac between there and Washington. Then combined, the two armies could have worked as one to bring about a Union victory.

But this Pope could not do. First, breaking off contact with the enemy could cause another instance where Pope lost track of the enemy, and that had already proven detrimental to Pope as evidenced by Jackson's march to Manassas Junction that concluded on August 27. Additionally, pulling back closer to Washington and abandoning more of northern Virginia went against Pope's command philosophy that he laid out to his superiors and his army when he arrived in the Eastern Theater.

Then, it seemingly fell to McClellan to effect the junction of the two armies once and for all. McClellan personally arrived in Alexandria across the Potomac River from Washington on the evening of August 26. Twenty-seven miles separated the two commanders. McClellan kept up a constant communication with Halleck on August 27. The confusion in intelligence that had plagued Halleck, Pope, and McClellan at this stage of the campaign reared its ugly head. McClellan's immediate concern was how to get the II and VI Corps of his army to Pope because he did not know where Pope's army was located. Worse yet, "I have no means of knowing the enemy's force between Pope and ourselves" due to the lack of cavalry.

Just twenty minutes after expressing these concerns, ominous news arrived from the front telling of the rout of Taylor's New Jersey brigade by an enemy force at Bull Run Bridge (see Chapter 5). In this episode, McClellan saw a small force—4,000 men—advanced into unknown territory prowled by a dangerous enemy force of unknown size get pounced upon without the benefit of being screened by cavalry and supported by artillery. "I think our policy now is to make these works perfectly safe and mobilize a couple of corps as soon as possible," McClellan advised Halleck, "but not to advance them until they can have their artillery and cavalry."

Minutes, then hours, ticked by as McClellan waited for a response from Halleck. The General-in-Chief told McClellan to "best act" as he saw fit to do. Then, Halleck relayed that "three-quarters of my time is taken up with the raising of new troops and matters in the West. I have no time for details. You

West Point graduate John G. Barnard served in various capacities as an engineer during the Civil War, including as chief engineer of the Department of Washington from 1861 to 1864. It was in this role that he warned both McClellan and Halleck near the end of August that the defenses of the capital were not nearly complete or as strong as some thought. (loc)

will therefore, as ranking general in the field, direct as you deem best; but at present orders for Pope's army should go through me." In this one dispatch, Halleck had left McClellan mostly to his own devices, told him he had no time for minor matters, and seemed to refute the notion that McClellan would have command of the combined armies.

The next day, Halleck was more explicit, ordering both Army of the Potomac corps with McClellan toward Manassas Junction. "Not a moment must be lost," Halleck urged. Franklin would go forward the next morning, August 29, and Sumner's would be prepared to march at a moment's notice.

By now, reports of Confederates at Manassas Junction had been confirmed. Without knowledge of Pope's whereabouts, Washingtonians worried that the enemy might advance on their city. John Barnard, chief engineer of the Washington fortifications, corresponded with both McClellan and Halleck, telling them that the defenses were imperfect. "A serious attack [against them] would not encounter a serious resistance," Barnard warned. Unfazed, Halleck sent a similar comment to Barnard that he did to McClellan: "I have no time for these details, and don't come to me until you exhaust other resources."

While messages raced back and forth across the Potomac, time was running out to connect the two Union armies. Ironically, on August 29, Lee's army reunited on the Manassas battlefield.

Perhaps recognizing the stress Halleck was under to complete his plan of concentration, President Lincoln tapped into the telegraph wires. "What news from direction of Manassas Junction?" he asked McClellan. "What generally?" With the lack of a clear picture of the operations in northern Virginia, Taylor's repulse at Bull Run Bridge, and Barnard's warning about the defenses of Washington, McClellan presented Lincoln with two feasible options. First, he advocated for concentrating "all our available forces to open communication with Pope," meaning a strong force, rather than a force of 4,000 men, would venture into the Virginia countryside to aid Pope and gather intelligence. Alternatively, McClellan wrote, they could "leave Pope to get out of his scrape & at once use all our means to make the Capital perfectly safe. No middle course will now answer," he concluded.

Leaving "Pope to get out of his scrape" particularly smacked Lincoln as bordering on treason, that McClellan hoped for Pope's demise. McClellan biographer Stephen W. Sears noted, though, that this "was a favorite figure of speech of" McClellan's, "one he used often and without particular malice, but Lincoln took it as expressing his true attitude toward his fellow general."

Despite Lincoln's disgust, following Pope's defeat on August 30, in which neither the II or VI Corps participated, and his withdrawal into Washington's defenses, Lincoln felt he had no one else to turn to who could quickly revive the demoralized Union army and face the immediate threat that the victorious Confederate army presented. McClellan received command of all the forces within the vicinity of Washington, supplanting Pope.

A dejected John Pope learned of this arrangement personally from McClellan on the afternoon of September 2 as he arrived within the city's fortifications with his army. Pope and his entourage were "covered with dust, their beards were powdered with it; they looked worn and serious, but alert and self-possessed." McClellan and Pope spoke briefly of the command arrangement. "Pope lifted his hat in a parting salute to McClellan and rode quietly on with his escort." Among Pope's former soldiers, word spread that they were now under McClellan's charge; cheers rent the air as Pope trotted off the stage of the Civil War's Eastern Theater.

In one month, Halleck's plan of concentrating two armies for one victory came unhinged. The personalities of Pope and McClellan—and, for that matter, Halleck, too—certainly played a role in the Federal defeat at Second Manassas. But personalities were not the only factor at play in late August 1862. Conflicting visions, objectives, intelligence, dearth of information, and expectations of command once the armies united pulled the pins out of Halleck's plan as much as the relationships of the three men tasked with implementing it. By bringing Halleck and Pope east, Lincoln and Stanton sought a streamlined command system in Virginia. This first attempt came to naught. In fact, they had to wait an additional 18 months for their visions to be realized.

How the Destruction of the Chantilly/ Ox Hill Battlefield Inspired the Modern Battlefield Preservation Movement

APPENDIX C

BY ED WENZEL

In the 1980s, developers in Maryland and Virginia little cared for historic resources. In the summer and fall of 1986, development threats at Antietam and Chantilly reached a crisis point. While historians and preservationists founded the Save Historic Antietam Foundation (SHAF) and rallied to fight off a shopping center, the same threats were also at work in Fairfax County, Virginia. There, county officials had already rezoned a large tract of land along Route 50, the site of the battle of Chantilly (Ox Hill), a bloody encounter fought in a thunderstorm at the end of the Second Manassas campaign. This tract was slated for intensive development, and construction was underway. There was little notice by anyone— that is, until two county residents observed what was going on.

One resident was Bud Hall, an FBI agent with a deep interest in the Civil War who often took runs through Ox Hill. One day he noticed two granite memorials to fallen Union generals at the battle, Isaac Stevens and Philip Kearny. Hall was shocked when he saw construction activity nearby. He at once investigated what this meant. The other individual was myself, back when I worked for the U.S. Geological Survey. As a part-time Civil War buff, I had only recently learned where the two monuments were located. Then, driving past one day, I too saw the construction activity and started asking questions. I contacted county officials, asking what preservation was being done. As I found out, the county was doing nothing. The battlefield would be developed, and the two monuments would be moved. I then called historian and author Brian Pohanka. Pohanka, outraged, pledged to help in any way possible.

What Hall and I discovered during our separate research was that in 1979, Fairfax County had offered 200 acres of the battlefield to the National Park Service, but the Park Service was not interested. This gave Fairfax supervisors an unspoken green light for

Early preservation efforts at Chantilly sought to mark the locations where Union Gens. Stevens and Kearny were mortally wounded. The boulders (left) and quartz (right) were placed by land owner and Confederate veteran John Ballard at the approximate location where Stevens fell in 1883 after Stevens's son marked the spot. (dw)

the property's development. By 1984, two builders had acquired most of the battlefield.

But what about the monuments? Fairfax planners envisioned that the elderly trustees who owned the monuments (and lived in New Jersey and West Virginia) could be persuaded to move them to a two-acre "historic park" to be proffered jointly by the Milton Company and the Centennial Development Corp. The park would straddle their boundary, but Milton soon backed out. Centennial then agreed to proffer both acres but would shift the park to a site along West Ox Road. Centennial would own the park, maintain the monuments, and interpret the battle. The new park would be 400 yards north of the monuments. Thankfully, the faux "historic park" never happened. By then, Hall had spoken to the trustees and urged them to fight the county and never give up the monuments.

I had also discovered that a Confederate soldier's grave had been found the previous year on the Milton Company property about 200 yards northwest of the monuments. Earthmoving machines had already cut 14 inches of earth from above the grave when a relic hunter detected uniform buttons. Just below the surface he extracted skull fragments, teeth, bones, and 10 South Carolina buttons (some with cloth still attached). He then carefully removed the bones and artifacts and took them to the coroner's office. Nothing was made public, and construction was never halted.

With this information verified, I called a reporter at the *Washington Post*, Barbara Carton, and asked if she knew that developers were building on a Civil War battlefield. Carton said, "No, I'm from Illinois. I'm not familiar with battlefields, but I'd like to do the story." A week later she got the go-ahead and scheduled an interview. Two days later, we met at the monuments and drove around the battlefield's construction sites. Three days after that, Carton called to say the story would be in the next day's paper.

On October 6, 1986, the Chantilly story appeared on the front-page of the *Post*. The news of the South Carolina soldier's bones laying forgotten on a storage shelf in the medical examiner's office was horrifying. The outrage was immediate, and the remains were later reinterred in South Carolina. During this time, the Associated Press picked up the story, and Civil War newsletters and periodicals reprinted it. The publicity generated by the Post's front-page story galvanized local Civil War buffs and historians, not to mention those where other battlefields were threatened.

Meanwhile, Hall, Pohanka, and I formed the Chantilly Battlefield Association (CBA) and engaged Fairfax County and Centennial in a series of meetings and discussions. The CBA made a presentation on the battle and insisted that the monuments stay exactly where they were, and that a county-owned battlefield park, however small, should be established to preserve the ground of Stevens's attack and the spot where he fell (near the monuments). Centennial agreed that moving the monuments made no sense. They would rework their plans and transfer the proffered two-acre park to the monument site. The new park would be under the management of the county Park Authority. In early 1987, the CBA began a petition drive for the county to purchase a two-and-a-half-acre parcel immediately adjacent to the land donated by Centennial. That land was the last fragment of the Chantilly/Ox Hill battlefield not in the developer's hands.

While the CBA fought to preserve something at Chantilly, Civil War historian Donald Pfanz, deeply affected by the tragedy, began to consider how a national preservation organization for Civil War battlefields might work. At Fredericksburg & Spotsylvania National Military Park, he discussed his idea with senior park staff who suggested he reach out to Pohanka. So, on April 22, 1987, Pfanz sent a two-page typewritten letter to Pohanka detailing how such an organization would operate. Pohanka responded immediately, noting that something had to be done at the national level or the Chantilly tragedy would be repeated. The two agreed that a meeting of like-minded individuals should be held with the object of forming a national preservation organization devoted solely to saving and protecting Civil War battlefields. Soon, the first such organization was created, the Association for the Preservation of Civil War Sites (APCWS).

Pfanz's letter to Pohanka became the "wellspring" of the modern Civil War battlefield preservation movement. With the loss of Chantilly, the APCWS forged ahead to build a membership-based organization that would acquire, protect, and preserve critical battlefield parcels before developers arrived. The APCWS succeeded far beyond anyone's expectations. After merging with the original (and competing) Civil War Trust in 1999, the new Civil

War Preservation Trust (CWPT) improved and streamlined its operations to boost acquisition of even more threatened ground. In 2011, the CWPT shortened its name to the Civil War Trust (CWT) and introduced a new logo. In 2014, the Trust launched an aggressive campaign to save endangered battlefields of the American Revolution and the War of 1812. Finally, in 2018, the Trust changed its name to the American Battlefield Trust (ABT) to better reflect its expanded mission. Today this organization has saved more than 57,000 acres of battlefield land in 25 states since 1987.

The tragic loss of most of the Ox Hill/Chantilly battlefield had an unforeseen silver lining. The near-complete destruction of Fairfax County's only major Civil War battlefield spurred private citizens to create what became a nationwide, award-winning education and preservation organization—one that works tirelessly to save, protect, and preserve hallowed ground sanctified by the blood of hundreds of thousands of American soldiers.

EDWARD T. WENZEL was born in Washington, D.C., and raised in Branchville, MD, and Falls Church, VA. Following high school, he joined the army and served in South Korea with the 528th MI Co., Eighth Army. He later worked 35 years in the field of topographic mapping with the U.S. Forest Service and U.S. Geological Survey. Ed is a member of the Bull Run Civil War Round Table and resides in Vienna, VA.

Second Manassas Campaign Driving Tours

APPENDIX D

Tour Stop 1—Cedar Mountain Battlefield

9465 General Winder Rd., Rapidan, VA 22733

Jackson's and Banks's forces clashed here on August 9, 1862 in what some consider to be the opening battle of the Second Manassas campaign. Jackson achieved a narrowly won tactical victory which was largely overshadowed by the poor command and control displayed during the battle and the high casualties his wing sustained to achieve it. The Cedar Mountain battlefield has been preserved by the American Battlefield Trust. Today, the Friends of Cedar Mountain Battlefield oversee the site of the first clash between John Pope and "Stonewall" Jackson. A half-mile interpretive trail carries you across the ground that saw the heaviest fighting on August 9, 1862.

➤ To Tour Stop 1A

If you wish to visit Verdiersville, site of the Federal raid that nearly nabbed Stuart and his staff on August 18, follow these directions. From the Friends of Cedar Mountain Battlefield office, turn left onto General Winder Rd. In 0.2 miles, turn left onto US-15 N. Drive 2.7 miles before turning right onto Rt. 601, Kettle Club Rd. Stay on Rt. 601 for 2.5 miles. Turn left onto Rt. 617, Winston Rd. In 1.1 miles, turn right onto US-522. Drive 7.4 miles. Then, turn left onto Pine Stake Rd. and remain on this road for 4.9 miles. Turn left onto Constitution Hwy. and make the first right onto Mine Run Rd. Pull over as soon as it is safe on Mine Run Rd. A historic marker marks the approximate location of Stuart's headquarters near Verdiersville.

➤ To Tour Stop 2

If you wish to forego the drive to Verdiersville, follow these directions to Stop 2, Remington. From the Friends of Cedar Mountain Battlefield office, turn left onto General Winder Rd. In 0.2 miles, turn left onto US-15 N. Drive 4.4 miles, then turn right to merge onto US-15 N/US-29 N toward Washington.

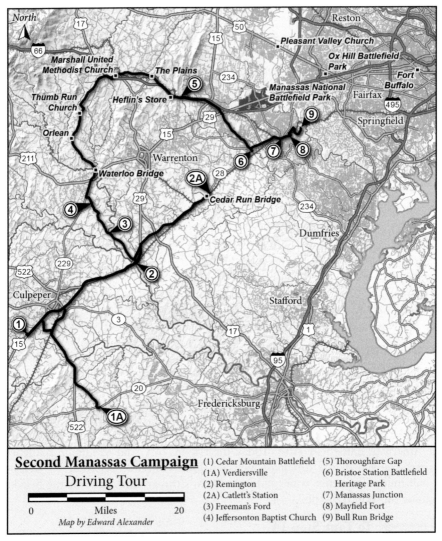

SECOND MANASSAS CAMPAIGN DRIVING TOUR—The Second Manassas Campaign stretched from the Rapidan River nearly to the Potomac River over the course of a few weeks in August 1862.

In 10.7 miles, turn right onto US-15 BUS N/US-29 BUS N. In 0.6 miles, make a right onto Hord Ave., followed by another quick right onto Willis Ave. Pull into the parking lot at the end of Willis Ave., exit your vehicle, and walk to a point where you are overlooking the Rappahannock River.

Tour Stop 1A–Verdiersville (alternate stop)

GPS: 38° 16.313′N, 77° 53.768′W

It was here at Catlett Rhoades's home on the morning of August 18 that Stuart and his staff were surprised and nearly captured by Thornton Brodhead's Federal cavalry. Brodhead's men not only snagged Stuart's cloak and plumed hat, but also valuable Confederate correspondence that alerted Pope to the planned Southern offensive against his left flank north of the Rapidan River. The Rhoades's homesite stood on the southwest corner of modern-day Constitution Hwy. and Mine Run Rd.

➤ To Tour Stop 2

To return to the main tour and head to the next stop, Remington, carefully turn around when it is safe to do so and return to Constitution Hwy. Turn left. In 0.4 miles, turn right onto Pine Stake Rd. Remain on this road for 4.9 miles, then turn right onto US-522. Travel on US-522 N for 10.9 miles, then turn right to merge onto US-15 N/US-29 N toward Washington. In 10.7 miles, turn right onto US-15 BUS N/US-29 BUS N. In 0.6 miles, make a right onto Hord Ave., followed by another quick right onto Willis Ave. Pull into the parking lot at the end of Willis Ave., exit your vehicle, and walk to a point where you are overlooking the Rappahannock River.

Tour Stop 2–Remington

12233 River Road, Remington, VA 22734

Prompted by the intelligence gathered by Brodhead, Pope pulled his army behind the Rappahannock River. Here at Rappahannock Station, Federal infantry and artillery guarded the bridge carrying the Orange and Alexandria Railroad over the river. A large artillery duel occurred here on August 23, and the Federals burned the bridge before moving in the direction of Warrenton.

➤ To Tour Stop 2A

If you wish to visit Catlett's Station, the site of J.E.B. Stuart's raid on the night of August 22-23, follow these directions. Depart the parking lot and travel straight onto River Rd. Make a slight right onto US-15 BUS N/US-29 BUS N/James Madison St. Drive 2 miles before turning right onto US-15 N/US-29 N. In 0.3 miles, turn right onto Rt. 28 N, Catlett Rd. In 10.5 miles on your right, you will see the site of the wartime bridge that carried the Orange & Alexandria Railroad over Cedar Run. Just beyond the bridge, make a right turn onto Old Catlett Rd. Drive 0.4 miles, followed by a right turn onto Rt. 806, Elk Run Rd. A Civil War Trails marker will be ahead on your right. Pull over and exit your vehicle.

➤ To Tour Stop 3

Depart the parking lot and travel straight onto River Rd. Make a slight right onto US-15 BUS N/US-29 BUS N/James Madison St. After 0.2 miles, turn left onto W Main St. At the stop light, continue straight onto Freeman's Ford Rd. In 4.8 miles, you will cross over the Rappahannock River and the wartime site of Freeman's Ford. Pull over onto the right shoulder of the road as soon as it is safe to do so.

Tour Stop 2A—Catlett's Station (alternate stop)

GPS: 38.652742, -77.639742

Stuart and 1,500 Confederate cavalrymen attacked the Federal garrison and Pope's headquarters train at Catlett's Station on the night of August 22-23. They attempted to burn the Orange and Alexandria Railroad bridge over Cedar Run, but a drenching rainstorm prevented them from doing so. Nonetheless, Stuart's men made off with valuable intelligence about the proximity of the Army of Virginia and the Army of the Potomac as well as Pope's uniform coat.

➤ To Tour Stop 3

Turn your vehicle around safely and drive 0.2 miles. Turn left onto Rt. 28 S, Catlett Rd. Drive 11.1 miles, then turn left onto US-15 S/US-29 S. In 4.8 miles, turn right onto Freeman's Ford Rd. In 4.8 miles, you will cross over the Rappahannock River and the wartime site of Freeman's Ford. Pull over onto the right shoulder of the road as soon as it is safe to do so.

Tour Stop 3—Freeman's Ford

GPS: 38.583049, -77.875724

Brigadier General Henry Bohlen's brigade was thrashed here by Confederates on August 22, and Bohlen himself was killed while trying to attack a Confederate wagon train. Confederate troops succeeded in driving the Federals back to the north bank of the Rappahannock River.

➤ To Tour Stop 4

Continue on Rt. 621 in the same direction your car is facing. Drive 3.2 miles, then stay to the left to remain on Rt. 621, Jeffersonton Rd. In 1.3 miles, when you are near the Jeffersonton United Methodist Church, you are in the area of Lee's headquarters at Jeffersonton. Drive 0.3 additional miles and pull into the driveway for Jeffersonton Baptist Church on your right.

The heights north of the Rappahannock River helped John Pope parry Robert E. Lee's multiple attempts to get across the river on August 22-23, 1862. (kp)

Tour Stop 4—Jeffersonton Baptist Church

18498 Springs Road, Jeffersonton, VA 22724

This crossroads town witnessed a meeting of the Army of Northern Virginia's high command on August 24. Lee met with his subordinates in a field just outside the town center and decided to divide his army in half, sending Jackson's men on a march around Pope's right flank to sever the Federals' line of supply and communication.

➡ To Tour Stop 5

Directions to the next tour stop will follow in the footsteps of Jackson's march (and later Longstreet's) around Pope on August 25-26 as much as the modern road network allows. Some of the roads are narrow, gravel roads, and there is one bridge that is a single lane 143 year old truss bridge. If you wish to proceed straight to Thoroughfare Gap on the most direct route, enter the address below into your GPS.

Turn left out of the driveway of Jeffersonton Baptist Church and continue straight on Rt. 621, Jeffersonton Rd. In 1.2 miles, turn right onto Rt. 229 N, Rixeyville Rd. Drive 2.2 miles before turning right onto US-211 E. Make an almost immediate left onto Rt. 622, Old Bridge Rd. Cross over the Waterloo Bridge. The current, 143 year old bridge sits on the original spans of the wartime bridge. Stuart's cavalry crossed here on their way to Catlett's Station on August 22. Federals burned the bridge on August 25, and Pvt. John Tribe, 5th New York Cavalry, received the Medal of Honor for his attempt to do so the previous day. Pope's right was in the area of Waterloo Bridge on August 25 when Jackson's column crossed the Rappahannock River four miles upstream (to your left as you cross the bridge) at Hinson's Mill Ford. Thus, the route you have traveled from Jeffersonton to here was not part of Jackson's march.

Continue on Leeds Manor Rd. for 3.7 miles to its intersection with Bears Den Rd. This is the approximate area where Jackson's column, after crossing at Hinson's Mill Ford to your left, entered today's Leeds Manor Rd. You will now be following in the footsteps of Jackson's foot cavalry (and subsequently Longstreet's trailing column) as best as modern roads allow. In 1.7 miles, you will pass through Orlean (Orleans in 1862), where Longstreet's column and army headquarters

Jeffersonton was a busy place before August 1862. Two roads intersected here: one carried travelers from the Shenandoah Valley to Falmouth while the other went from Washington, DC, to Milledgeville, Georgia. Work on Jeffersonton Baptist Church began in 1848. Though the building caught fire in 1877, the walls you see today are the wartime walls. (kp)

Heflin's Store, built in 1845, still stands in Little Georgetown. The entire Army of Northern Virginia passed this structure in August 1862. (kp)

bivouacked on the night of the 26th. In Orlean at 1.7 miles, turn right onto Rt. 732, John Barton Payne Rd. In 3.3 miles, make a slight left onto Tanner Branch Rd. Shortly on your left, you will find Thumb Run Church, a wartime structure that Jackson's column passed on August 25. The Confederates continued down Tanner Branch Rd., which dead ends today. Return to Rt. 732, John Barton Payne Rd., and turn left. In 0.8 miles, make a left turn to stay onto Rt. 733, Wilson Rd. In 0.6 miles, turn right onto Rt. 647, Crest Hill Rd. In 1.4 miles, you are in the area where a detachment of the 9th New York Cavalry nearly captured or killed Lee on August 27. After driving another 4.0 miles, you will have passed first Big Cobbler, then Little Cobbler Mountain. Somewhere in this vicinity is where Jackson stood upon a rock outcropping and watched his troops march, as related in Chapter 4. Continue for another 2 miles to make a left on Free State Rd. In 0.3 miles, Free State Rd. becomes US-17 BUS S. In 0.4 miles, turn right into the parking lot of Marshall United Methodist Church. Jackson's column stopped its march in the area of Marshall (wartime Salem) after trekking more than 25 miles on August 25. Here, you will also find a historic marker explaining Lee's escape near Ada on August 27.

Turn right onto W Main St. In 4.8 miles, you have entered The Plains, known as White Plains at the time of the Civil War. There is a Civil War Trails sign at the four way stop in the middle of the town describing Longstreet's column passing through here on August 28. In 2.0 miles, you will pass the entrance road to Avenel, where Robert E. Lee stayed on the night of August 28. The home is privately owned; do not trespass. In 1.4 miles, turn right onto Rt. 628, Blantyre Rd. Drive 0.3 miles to turn left onto Rt. 674, Trapp Branch Rd., placing you once again on the original route of Jackson's and Longstreet's march. You are passing through Little Georgetown. The building almost immediately on your left as you turn onto Trapp Branch Rd. is Heflin's Store, a building constructed in 1845. In 0.6 miles, turn right onto Rt. 55, John Marshall Hwy. In 1.7 miles, after you have passed through Thoroughfare Gap, make a left onto Rt. 723, Turner Rd. In 0.1 miles, turn left onto Beverley Mill Dr. In 0.8 miles, park your car in the designated parking area. Exit your vehicle and walk in the same direction you were driving to the Civil War Trails sign.

Thoroughfare Gap's significance can still be seen today, though the intrusion of Interstate 66 through the battlefield has segmented the battlefield significantly for visitors. (kp)

17502 Beverley Mill Drive, Broad Run, VA 20137

This pass in the Bull Run Mountains witnessed Jackson's column march through it unopposed on August 26 while Longstreet's men fought to hold it against an outnumbered Federal force on August 28. Trails in the Bull Run Mountains Natural Area Preserve bring you to the quarry trench fought over by the opposing forces and a climb up Mother Leathercoat Mountain. The trails are open Friday through Sunday. Chapman's Mill, a witness to the Civil War, is open on Saturdays and Sundays.

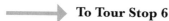 **To Tour Stop 6**

Proceed out the way you drove in on Beverley Mill Dr. Turn right onto Rt. 723, Turner Rd., followed by a left onto Rt. 55, John Marshall Hwy. Stay on this road, which turns into Rt. 619, Linton Hall Rd., for 11.1 miles. Then, turn right onto Iron Brigade Unit Ave. At the roundabout, take the third exit into the parking lot of Bristoe Station Battlefield Heritage Park.

Tour Stop 6—Bristoe Station Battlefield Heritage Park

Iron Brigade Unit Avenue and Tenth Alabama Way, Bristow, VA 20136

Jackson's column cut the Orange and Alexandria Railroad here on August 26, 1862, and Richard Ewell's division fought Joseph Hooker's Federals here the next day at the battle of Kettle Run. Ewell's forces withdrew toward Manassas after receiving Jackson's orders to not become entangled in an engagement with the Federals, after several hours of fighting at Bristoe Station. Prince William County's Office of Historic Preservation manages the 140-acre battlefield park, site of two engagements during the Civil War on August 27, 1862, and October 14, 1863. The 1861-1862 trail, 1.3 miles long, brings you to the Kettle Run battlefield and covers Jackson's attack on Bristoe Station on the night of August 26. The park is open daily dawn to dusk and guided tours are offered on the second and fourth weekends of the month, May through October.

→ To Tour Stop 7

Exit the parking lot and turn right onto Iron Brigade Unit Ave. Turn left onto Rt. 619, Bristow Rd. In 0.3 miles, turn right onto Chapel Springs Rd. In another 0.3 miles, turn right onto Rt. 28 N. As you drive on this road, you are paralleling the historic Orange & Alexandria Railroad (on your right), the route that Jackson's troops took from Bristoe Station to Manassas Junction. In 4.0 miles, turn right onto West St. Cross the railroad tracks and turn left into the train depot parking lot. An interpretive sign on the opposite end of the parking lot from where you entered discusses Jackson's raid on Manassas Junction.

Tour Stop 7—Manassas Junction

9431 West Street, Manassas, VA 20110

Jackson's Confederates looted the Federal stores here on August 27, 1862, after capturing the important supply depot the previous night. Interpretive signs can be found in front of the Manassas Museum and Manassas Visitor Center. The actual junction still exists today at GPS: 38.749364, -77.486825.

→ To Tour Stop 8

Retrace your route on West St. Turn right onto Center St. In 0.3 miles, stay to the left on Rt. 28, Zebedee St. Make the first right onto Quarry Rd. In 0.6 miles, turn right to remain on Quarry Rd. Drive another 0.3 miles to turn right onto Battery Heights Blvd. The parking lot for Mayfield Fort will be immediately on your left.

Tour Stop 8—Mayfield Fort

8401 Quarry Road, Manassas, VA 20110

Confederates used the extensive fortifications around Manassas Junction constructed in 1861, like Mayfield Fort, to defeat George Taylor's New Jersey brigade during the battle of Bull Run Bridge on August 27, 1862. Taylor's brigade advanced to the area of the Home Depot on Liberia Avenue (visible from Mayfield Fort) before being driven back to Bull Run Bridge. A handful of interpretive signs about the August 1862 battle can be found within the existing fortifications.

To Tour Stop 9

Turn right out of the parking lot, followed by another right onto Quarry Rd. Turn left onto Liberia Ave. In 0.3 miles, turn right onto Euclid Ave. The advance of Taylor's New Jersey brigade apexed near here on August 27. In 0.6 miles, turn right onto Conner Dr., followed by the second left into a parking lot. The wartime Conner House was a witness to the Battle of Bull Run Bridge. Return to Euclid Ave. and turn right. In 0.3 miles, turn right onto Manassas Dr. Continue for 2.0 miles, then turn right into Blooms Park.

Tour Stop 9–Bull Run Bridge

9701 Manassas Drive, Manassas Park, VA 20111

Blooms Park is the site where Taylor's brigade deployed into their battle lines and later were defeated by Jackson's men. Trails lead through the park, including one down a steep decline to Bull Run, where the original abutments of the bridge that carried the Orange and Alexandria Railroad over the stream can be seen.

Battles of Second Manassas and Chantilly Driving Tour

Tour Stop 1–Brawner Farm

6501 Pageland Lane, Gainesville, VA 20155

The opening shots of the battle of Second Manassas were fired on the farm of John Brawner on the evening of August 28, 1862. This fight was one of the most brutal of the war, and the Federals withdrew from the field after nightfall. A 1.6 mile hike, the Brawner Farm Loop Trail, allows visitors to walk along the Union and Confederate battlelines during the intense firefight. The interpretive center is open seasonally and has exhibits about the battle of Second Manassas.

To Tour Stop 1A

Exit the parking lot and turn left onto Pageland Ln. At the traffic light, turn left onto US-29 N, Lee Hwy. In 0.9 miles, the entrance to the Battery Heights parking lot will be on your left.

To Tour Stop 2

Exit the parking lot and turn left onto Pageland Ln. At the traffic light, turn left onto US-29 N, Lee Hwy. Drive 2.7 miles. The Stone House parking lot will be on the left just past the Lee Hwy.-Sudley Rd. intersection.

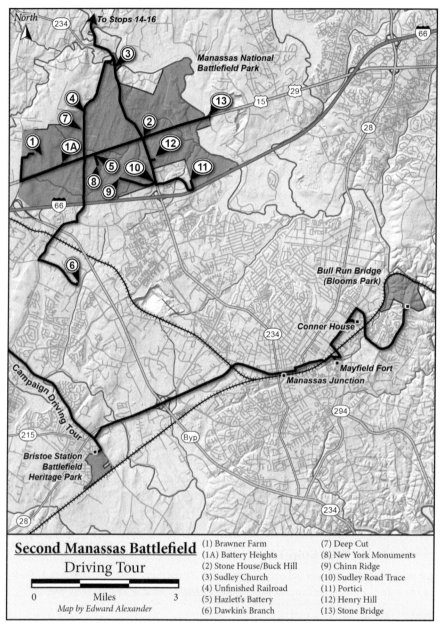

Second Manassas Battlefield

Driving Tour

0   Miles   3

Map by Edward Alexander

(1) Brawner Farm
(1A) Battery Heights
(2) Stone House/Buck Hill
(3) Sudley Church
(4) Unfinished Railroad
(5) Hazlett's Battery
(6) Dawkin's Branch
(7) Deep Cut
(8) New York Monuments
(9) Chinn Ridge
(10) Sudley Road Trace
(11) Portici
(12) Henry Hill
(13) Stone Bridge

SECOND MANASSAS BATTLEFIELD DRIVING TOUR—While much of the land where the battle of Second Manassas was fought has been incorporated into Manassas National Battlefield, the sites of the clashes around Manassas Junction are in various states of preservation. Some of the landscape and roadways from 1862 still remain, however.

Tour Stop 1A—Battery Heights

GPS: 38.811438, -77.557214

Battery Heights (GPS coordinates in caption to August 29 marker): Union and Confederate artillery utilized this high ground during the battle's three days. Confederate artillery positioned here helped cut up the Federal attack against the Deep Cut on August 30.

Tour Stop 2—Stone House/Buck Hill

GPS: 38.819101, -77.525082

John Pope's headquarters were established on Buck Hill during the battle, the eminence behind the wartime Stone House. Henry Matthews and his wife Jane owned the building during the war, which was used as a hospital following the Second Manassas battle. Graffiti of soldiers treated there can still be seen on the upstairs floorboards. The house is open seasonally for tours by Manassas National Battlefield. A short walking trail leads to the top of Buck Hill and provides Pope's vantage point of the battlefield.

➤ To Tour Stop 3

Turn right out of the Stone House parking lot, then make an immediate right at the traffic light onto Rt. 234, Sudley Rd. Drive 1.6 miles. The small National Park Service parking lot on your left is Tour Stop 3.

Tour Stop 3—Sudley Church

GPS: 38.838821, -77.537417

This area was the extreme left of Jackson's battle line held by A. P. Hill's infantry and Fitzhugh Lee's cavalry. The wartime church stood on the site of the modern church, which was constructed in 1922, with an addition added in 1992. The graves of Col. Daniel Ledbetter and Capt. Miles Norton of Orr's South Carolina Rifles can be found in the adjacent cemetery. Both died as a result of the nearby fighting on August 29, 1862.

➤ To Tour Stop 4

Carefully turn left onto Rt. 234, Sudley Rd. In 0.2 miles, turn left onto Featherbed Ln. In 1.3 miles, the Unfinished Railroad parking lot will be on your left.

Tour Stop 4—Unfinished Railroad

GPS: 38.825586, -77.548660

Jackson anchored his line along and behind the unfinished grade of the Independent Line of the Manassas Gap Railroad. Although cuts and grades were constructed for the line, due to financial setbacks and the outbreak of the war, tracks were never laid here. This section of the rail line is most famous for the fighting along it on August 29-30, 1862. A 1.2 mile trail that leaves from the parking lot brings you to the site of many of the Federal attacks on August 29.

➤ To Tour Stop 5

Exit the parking lot by turning left onto Featherbed Ln. Drive 0.9 miles and turn left at the stop sign onto US-29 N, Lee Hwy. In 0.2 miles, turn right onto the tour road and park in the spaces immediately on your right.

Tour Stop 5—Hazlett's Battery

GPS: 38.813342, -77.544764

At least six Union batteries occupied this knoll during the fighting on August 29-30. John Hatch's and John Hood's opposing divisions fought here around Groveton in the growing darkness of August 29. Part of Hood's reconnaissance ordered by Longstreet, the intelligence gleaned from the fighting did not provide Lee the answers he hoped to find.

➤ To: Tour Stop 6

Exit the parking lot and turn left onto US-29 S, Lee Hwy. In 0.2 miles, turn left onto Groveton Rd. In 1.3 miles, at the traffic light, turn right onto Balls Ford Rd. In 1.0 mile, turn left onto Wellington Rd. This road generally follows the wartime Manassas-Gainesville Rd. In 1.0 mile, turn left onto Tac Ct. followed by an immediate right into the business parking lot. Exit your vehicle and walk to the historic marker along Wellington Rd.

Fitz John Porter's V Corps first came into contact with James Longstreet's troops on August 29, 1862, near here. Once in contact, the next 24 hours proved harrowing for Porter, more so from dealing with and trying to understand John Pope's orders than with the Confederates in his front. (dw)

Tour Stop 6—Dawkin's Branch

GPS: 38.776196, -77.550951

Fitz John Porter's Fifth Corps ran into elements of James Longstreet's arriving Confederates here on August 29. The area has been built up considerably, but one historical marker details the story of Porter, his men, and the subsequent 24 year battle over the charges Pope leveled at Porter as a result of him not attacking here.

To Tour Stop 7

Exit the parking lot and turn left onto Tac Ct. Turn right onto Wellington Rd. In 1.0 mile, turn right onto Balls Ford Rd. Travel 1.2 miles before turning left onto Groveton Rd. In 1.3 miles, continue straight across US-29, Lee Hwy. In 0.6 miles, the Deep Cut parking lot will be on your left.

Tour Stop 7 – Deep Cut

GPS: 38.820792, -77.549286

The largest Federal attack of the battle occurred here on the afternoon of August 30, 1862. Ultimately, Fitz John Porter's 6,000-plus attackers were repulsed in some of the heaviest fighting of the battle. Follow the trail to see the monument dedicated to the Federal dead of Second Manassas, which was dedicated in 1865. Several other interpretive markers can be found along the railroad embankment describing this assault.

To Tour Stop 8

Turn right onto Featherbed Ln. In 0.6 miles, turn left at the stop sign onto US-29 N, Lee Hwy. In 0.2 miles, turn right onto the tour road. Proceed past the first parking area on your right where you stopped earlier. Drive to the end of the road and park in the lot next to two monuments.

Tour Stop 8 – New York Monuments

GPS: 38.810309, -77.544063

The 5th and 10th New York first met Longstreet's 25,000 men here in one of the largest attacks of the Civil War. The two regiments paid dearly for their stand against overwhelming numbers, especially the 5th New York. The monuments were dedicated in 1906. A trail behind the monuments will take you in the footsteps of the Confederate assault as it made its way towards Chinn Ridge.

To Tour Stop 9

Retrace your drive back to US-29, and turn right. In 1.0 mile at the traffic light, turn right onto Rt. 234, Sudley Rd. In 0.5 miles, turn right onto the park tour road. Make another right in 0.7 miles. The Chinn Ridge parking lot is at the end of the road.

Tour Stop 9—Chinn Ridge

GPS: 38.806714, -77.535122

For 90 minutes, successive Union brigades fended off Longstreet's attackers here on Chinn Ridge to buy time for a final Federal defensive line to be established. A one mile trail tells the story of the fight for Chinn Ridge, and a new extension to the trail allows visitors to walk in the footsteps of the Confederate attacks against Henry Hill and the Sudley Road line after they conquered Chinn Ridge.

→ To Tour Stop 10

Proceed back in the direction you just drove. In 0.7 miles, just before the tour road's intersection with Sudley Rd., park in the small gravel lot on the left side of the road. Exit your vehicle and follow the brown signs and path to a National Park Service interpretive wayside in the historic trace of the wartime Sudley Rd.

Tour Stop 10—Sudley Road Trace

GPS: 38.80564, -77.52206

Today's Sudley Road does not follow the roadway's original trace, which can be located today by following the road cut, power lines, and reconstructed fences. Union soldiers used the roadway to slow down the Confederate attack on August 30 until darkness allowed the army to withdraw across Bull Run.

→ To Tour Stop 11

Proceed onto the tour road and make an immediate right onto Rt. 234, Sudley Rd. Make a left at the next light onto Battleview Pkwy. Drive 0.8 miles and turn left onto Rock Rd. Follow Rock Rd. to the Portici parking lot.

Tour Stop 11—Portici

GPS: 38.806263, -77.508550

The Lewis family home stood here on August 30 and witnessed the largest cavalry engagement of the Civil War to date. Confederate cavalry attempted to cut off Pope's retreat across Bull Run, but John Buford's Federal horsemen slowed them down before being overwhelmed. In the end, the Confederate cavalry did not hamper the Union withdrawal. The house burned down in late 1862. However, by taking the mowed path from the parking lot you can walk out to the house site.

→ To Tour Stop 12

Return to Battleview Pkwy. In 0.8 miles, turn right onto Rt. 234, Sudley Rd. In 0.5 miles, turn right into the Henry Hill Visitor Center parking lot.

Tour Stop 12—Henry Hill

6511 Sudley Rd, Manassas, VA 20109

Famous for the fighting that occurred here during the battle of First Manassas on July 21, 1861, this hill and the Sudley Road were John Pope's and his army's last stand on the evening of August 30. The interpretive trail and markers atop Henry Hill today discuss the 1861 fighting, but the hillside nonetheless played just as important a role in 1862 as it did the previous year.

To Tour Stop 13

Exit the parking lot and turn right onto Rt. 234, Sudley Rd. In 0.5 miles, turn right onto US-29 N, Lee Hwy. In 1.4 miles, just after crossing Bull Run, turn left into the Stone Bridge parking lot.

Tour Stop 13—Stone Bridge

GPS: 38.825007, -77.501330

Retreating Confederate troops blew up the Stone Bridge, which carried the Warrenton Turnpike across Bull Run, in March 1862. Federal engineers used the existing abutments to construct a span here that, on the night of August 30, 1862, carried John Pope's defeated Army of Virginia to Centreville four miles to the east. The current structure was built in 1884.

To Tour Stop 14

This portion of the tour will follow "Stonewall" Jackson's column on August 31, 1862. Turn right onto US-29 S, Lee Hwy. In 1.4 miles, turn right onto Rt. 234, Sudley Rd. In 2.3 miles, turn right onto Rt. 659, Gum Spring Rd. In 6.7 miles, turn right onto US-50 E, John Mosby Hwy. In 3.4 miles, Pleasant Valley United Methodist Church will be on your right.

Tour Stop 14—Pleasant Valley United Methodist Church

43987 John Mosby Hwy., Chantilly, VA

Lee dispatched Jackson to turn the Federal position at Centreville on August 31. Jackson's march began at Sudley Springs and ended here at Pleasant Valley Church. The next morning, his men continued marching down the Little River Turnpike towards Fairfax Courthouse.

To Tour Stop 15

Turn right onto US-50 E, John Mosby Hwy. In 6.9 miles, take the W Ox Rd. S exit and merge onto W Ox Rd. In 0.2 miles, just past the traffic light, turn right into Ox Hill Battlefield Park.

Tour Stop 15—Ox Hill Battlefield Park

4134 West Ox Road, Fairfax, VA 22033

The last battle of the campaign was fought here at Ox Hill during a driving thunderstorm. Union generals Isaac Stevens and Phil Kearny were killed in two separate attacks, and Jackson's turning movement came to an end. Though mostly lost to development, an event that led to the foundation of the strong battlefield preservation movement today, the battlefield park features excellent interpretive waysides and a few monuments along the short walking trail.

Tour Stop 16—Fort Buffalo

GPS: 38.870260, -77.157137

Near here on September 2, John Pope and George McClellan met, and McClellan informed Pope that all the Federal forces near Washington fell under his command, subordinating Pope to McClellan. Nothing remains of Fort Buffalo today, and the only thing noting its location is the Virginia Department of Historic Resources marker.

Order of Battle

THE BATTLE OF SECOND MANASSAS

ARMY OF NORTHERN VIRGINIA
General Robert E. Lee

RIGHT WING Maj. Gen. James Longstreet
ANDERSON'S DIVISION Maj. Gen. Richard H. Anderson
Armistead's Brigade Brig. Gen. Lewis A. Armistead
9th Virginia • 14th Virginia • 38th Virginia • 53rd Virginia • 57th Virginia
5th Virginia Battalion

Mahone's Brigade Brig. Gen. William Mahone
6th Virginia • 12th Virginia • 16th Virginia • 41st Virginia

Wright's Brigade Brig. Gen. Ambrose R. Wright
44th Alabama • 3rd Georgia • 22nd Georgia • 48th Georgia

JONES'S DIVISION Brig. Gen. David R. Jones
Toombs's Brigade Col. Henry L. Benning
2nd Georgia • 15th Georgia • 17th Georgia • 20th Georgia

Drayton's Brigade Brig. Gen. Thomas F. Drayton
50th Georgia • 51st Georgia • 15th South Carolina • Phillip's (GA) Legion

Jones's Brigade Col. George T. Anderson
1st Georgia • 7th Georgia • 8th Georgia • 9th Georgia • 11th Georgia

WILCOX'S DIVISION Brig. Gen. Cadmus Wilcox
Wilcox's Brigade Brig. Gen. Cadmus Wilcox
8th Alabama • 9th Alabama • 10th Alabama • 11th Alabama

Pryor's Brigade Brig. Gen. Roger A. Pryor
14th Alabama • 2nd Florida • 5th Florida • 8th Florida • 3rd Virginia

Featherston's Brigade Brig. Gen. Winfield Scott Featherston
12th Mississippi • 16th Mississippi • 19th Mississippi
2nd Mississippi Battalion

Artillery
Thomas Artillery (VA) • Dixie Artillery (VA)

HOOD'S DIVISION Brig. Gen. John B. Hood
Hood's Brigade Brig. Gen. John B. Hood
18th Georgia • Hampton Legion • 1st Texas • 4th Texas • 5th Texas

Law's Brigade Col. Evander M. Law
4th Alabama • 2nd Mississippi • 11th Mississippi • 6th North Carolina

Artillery Maj. B. W. Frobel
German Artillery (SC) • Palmetto Artillery (SC) • Rowan Artillery (NC)

Evans's Independent Brigade Brig. Gen. Nathan G. Evans
17th South Carolina • 18th South Carolina • 22nd South Carolina (detached)
23rd South Carolina • Holcombe Legion • Macbeth Artillery (SC)

KEMPER'S DIVISION Brig. Gen. James L. Kemper
Kemper's Brigade Col. Montgomery D. Corse
1st Virginia • 7th Virginia • 11th Virginia • 17th Virginia • 24th Virginia

Pickett's Brigade Col. Eppa Hunton
8th Virginia • 18th Virginia • 19th Virginia • 28th Virginia • 56th Virginia

Jenkins's Brigade Brig. Gen. Micah Jenkins
1st South Carolina • 2nd South Carolina (Rifles) • 4th South Carolina Battalion
5th South Carolina • 6th South Carolina • Palmetto Sharpshooters

Artillery
Washington Artillery (LA) Col. J. B. Walton
1st Company • 2nd Company • 3rd Company • 4th Company

Lee's Battalion Col. Stephen D. Lee
Bath Artillery • Portsmouth Artillery (VA) • Bedford Artillery (VA)
Parker's Battery (VA) • Taylor's Battery (VA) • Rhett's Battery (SC)

Miscellaneous Batteries
Norfolk Artillery (VA) • Goochland Artillery (VA) • Donaldsonville Artillery (LA)
Moorman's Battery (VA) • Loudoun Artillery (VA) • Fauquier Artillery (VA)

LEFT WING Maj. Gen. Thomas J. Jackson
JACKSON'S DIVISION Brig. Gen. W. B. Taliaferro
"Stonewall" Brigade Col. William S. H. Baylor
2nd Virginia • 4th Virginia • 5th Virginia 27th Virginia • 33rd Virginia

Second Brigade Col. Bradley T. Johnson
1st Virginia Battalion • 21st Virginia • 42nd Virginia • 48th Virginia

Third Brigade Col. Alexander G. Taliaferro
47th Alabama • 48th Alabama • 10th Virginia • 23rd Virginia • 37th Virginia

Fourth Brigade Brig. Gen. William E. Starke
1st Louisiana • 2nd Louisiana • 9th Louisiana • 10th Louisiana
15th Louisiana • Coppen's Louisiana Battalion

Artillery Maj. L. M. Shumaker
Alleghany Artillery (VA) • Baltimore Artillery (MD) • Danville Artillery (VA)
Hampden Artillery (VA) • Lee Artillery (VA) • Rice's Battery (VA)
Rockbridge Artillery (VA) • Winchester Battery (VA)

LIGHT DIVISION Maj. Gen. A. P. Hill
Branch's Brigade Brig. Gen. Lawerence O. Branch
7th North Carolina • 18th North Carolina • 28th North Carolina
33rd North Carolina • 37th North Carolina

Archer's Brigade Brig. Gen. James J. Archer
5th Alabama Battalion • 19th Georgia • 1st Tennessee (Provisional Army)
7th Tennessee • 14th Tennessee

Pender's Brigade Brig. Gen. William D. Pender
16th North Carolina • 22nd North Carolina • 34th North Carolina
38th North Carolina

Field's Brigade Brig. Gen. Charles W. Field
40th Virginia • 47th Virginia • 55th Virginia • 22nd Virginia Battalion

Gregg's Brigade Brig. Gen. Maxcy Gregg
1st South Carolina • 1st South Carolina (Orr's Rifles) • 12th South Carolina
13th South Carolina • 14th South Carolina

Thomas's Brigade Col. Edward L. Thomas
14th Georgia • 35th Georgia • 45th Georgia • 49th Georgia

Artillery Lt. Col. Reuben L. Walker
Fredericksburg Artillery (VA) • Crenshaw's Battery (VA) • Letcher Artillery (VA)
Middlesex Artillery (VA) • Branch Artillery (NC) • Pee Dee Artillery (SC)
Purcell Artillery (VA)

EWELL'S DIVISION Maj. Gen. Richard S. Ewell
Lawton's Brigade Brig. Gen. A.R. Lawton
13th Georgia • 26th Georgia • 31st Georgia • 38th Georgia • 60th Georgia
61st Georgia

Trimble's Brigade Brig. Gen. Issac R. Trimble
15th Alabama • 12th Georgia • 21st Georgia • 21st North Carolina
1st North Carolina Battalion

Hays's Brigade Col. Henry Forno
5th Louisiana • 6th Louisiana • 7th Louisiana • 8th Louisiana • 14th Louisiana

Early's Brigade Brig. Gen. Jubal A. Early
13th Virginia • 25th Virginia • 31st Virginia • 44th Virginia • 49th Virginia
52nd Virginia • 58th Virginia

Artillery
Staunton Artillery (VA) • Chesapeake Artillery (MD) • Louisiana Guard Artillery
1st Maryland Battery • Johnson's Battery (VA) • Courtney Artillery (VA)

CAVALRY DIVISION Maj. Gen. J. E. B. Stuart
Robertson's Brigade Brig. Gen. Beverly H. Robertson
2nd Virginia • 6th Virginia • 7th Virginia • 12th Virginia
17th Virginia Battalion

Lee's Brigade Brig. Gen. Fitzhugh Lee
1st Virginia • 3rd Virginia • 4th Virginia • 5th Virginia • 9th Virginia

Artillery
Virginia Battery (Stuart Horse Artillery)

ARMY OF THE POTOMAC
Maj. Gen. George B. McClellan

THIRD CORPS Maj. Gen. Samuel P. Heintzelman
Headquarters Escort
5th New Cavalry (3 cos.)

FIRST DIVISION Maj. Gen. Philip Kearny
First Brigade Brig. Gen. John C. Robinson
20th Indiana • 30th Ohio (6 cos.) • 63rd Pennsylvania • 105th Pennsylvania

Second Brigade Brig. Gen. David B. Birney
3rd Maine • 4th Maine • 1st New York • 38th New York • 40th New York
101st New York • 57th Pennsylvania

Third Brigade Col. Orlando M. Poe
37th New York • 99th Pennsylvania • 2nd Michigan • 3rd Michigan
5th Michigan

Artillery
Battery E, 1st Rhode Island • Battery K, 1st United States

SECOND DIVISION Maj. Gen. Joseph Hooker
First Brigade Brig. Gen. Cuvier Grover
2nd New Hampshire • 1st Massachusetts • 11th Massachusetts
16th Massachusetts • 26th Pennsylvania

Second Brigade Col. Nelson Taylor
70th New York • 71st New York • 72nd New York • 73rd New York
74th New York

Third Brigade Col. Joseph B. Carr
2nd New York • 5th New Jersey • 6th New Jersey • 7th New Jersey
8th New Jersey • 115th Pennsylvania

Artillery
6th Maine Battery

FIFTH CORPS Maj. Gen. Fitz John Porter
First Division Maj. Gen. George W. Morell
First Brigade Col. Charles W. Roberts
2nd Maine • 18th Massachusetts • 22nd Massachusetts • 13th New York
25th New York • 1st Michigan

Second Brigade Brig. Gen. Charles Griffin
9th Massachusetts • 32nd Massachusetts • 14th New York • 62nd Pennsylvania
4th Michigan

Third Brigade Brig. Gen. Daniel Butterfield
12th New York • 17th New York • 44th New York • 83rd Pennsylvania
16th Michigan • 1st U.S. Sharpshooters

Artillery
3rd Massachusetts • Battery C, 1st Rhode Island • Battery D, 5th United States

SECOND DIVISION Brig. Gen. George Sykes
First Brigade Lt. Col. Robert C. Buchanan
3rd United States • 4th United States • 12th United States (1st Battalion)
14th United States (1st Battalion) • 14th United States (2nd Battalion)

Second Brigade Lt. Col. William Chapman
Company G, 1st United States • 2nd United States • 6th United States
10th United States • 11th United States • 17th United States

Third Brigade Col. Gouverneur K. Warren
5th New York • 10th New York

Artillery Capt. Stephen H. Weed
Batteries E and G, 1st United States • Battery I, 5th United States
Battery K, 5th United States

RESERVE CORPS Brig. Gen. Samuel D. Sturgis
Piatt's Brigade Brig. Gen. A. Sanders Piatt
63rd Indiana (4 companies) • 86th New York

NINTH CORPS Maj. Gen. Jesse L. Reno
FIRST DIVISION Maj. Gen. Isaac I. Stevens

First Brigade Col. Benjamin C. Christ
50th Pennsylvania • 8th Michigan

Second Brigade Col. Daniel Leasure
46th New York (5 cos.) • 100th Pennsylvania

Third Brigade Col. Addison Farnsworth
28th Massachusetts • 79th New York

Artillery
Battery E, 2nd United States

SECOND DIVISION Maj. Gen. Jesse L. Reno
First Brigade Col. James Nagle
6th New Hampshire • 48th Pennsylvania • 2nd Maryland

Second Brigade Col. Edward Ferrero
21st Massachusetts • 51st New York • 51st Pennsylvania

Artillery
Battery D, Pennsylvania Light Artillery • 2nd New York Light Artillery

ARMY OF VIRGINIA
Maj. Gen. John Pope

Headquarters Escort
1st Ohio Cavalry (Cos. A & C) • 5th New York Cavalry (7 cos.) • 36th Ohio

FIRST CORPS Maj. Gen. Franz Sigel
Headquarters Escort
1st Indiana Cavalry (Cos. I & K)

FIRST DIVISION Brig. Gen. Robert C. Schenck
First Brigade Brig. Gen. Julius Stahel
8th New York • 41st New York • 45th New York • 27th Pennsylvania

Second Brigade Col. Nathaniel C. McLean
25th Ohio • 55th Ohio • 73rd Ohio • 75th Ohio

Artillery
Battery K, 1st Ohio Artillery • 2nd New York Light

SECOND DIVISION Brig. Gen. Adolph von Steinwehr
First Brigade Col. John A. Koltes
29th New York • 68th New York • 73rd Pennsylvania

THIRD DIVISION Brig. Gen. Carl Schurz
First Brigade Col. Alexander Schimmelfenning
61st Ohio • 74th Pennsylvania • 8th West Virginia
Battery F, Pennsylvania Artillery

Second Brigade Col. Wlodzimierz Krzyzanowski
54th New York • 58th New York • 75th Pennsylvania
Battery L, 2nd New York Artillery

Independent Brigade Brig. Gen. Robert H. Milroy
2nd West Virginia • 3rd West Virginia • 5th West Virginia • 82nd Ohio
Troops C, E, and L, 1st West Virginia Cavalry • 12th Ohio Battery

Cavalry Brigade Col. John Beardsley
1st Connecticut Battalion • 1st Maryland • 4th New York • 9th New York
6th Ohio

Reserve Artillery Capt. Louis Schirmer
Battery I, 1st New York Light • 13th New York • Battery C, West Virginia Artillery

Unattached
Troop C, 3rd West Virginia Cavalry

THIRD CORPS Maj. Gen. Irvin McDowell
First Division Brig. Gen. Rufus King
First Brigade Brig. Gen. John P. Hatch
22nd New York • 24th New York • 30th New York • 84th New York (14th Militia)
2nd United States Sharpshooters

Second Brigade Brig. Gen. Abner Doubleday
56th Pennsylvania • 76th New York • 95th New York

Third Brigade Brig. Gen. Marsena R. Patrick
21st New York • 23rd New York • 35th New York • 80th New York (20th Militia)

Fourth Brigade Brig. Gen. John Gibbon
2nd Wisconsin • 6th Wisconsin • 7th Wisconsin • 19th Indiana

Artillery
1st New Hampshire • Battery D, 1st Rhode Island • Battery L, 1st New York
Battery B, 4th United States

Second Division Brig. Gen. James B. Ricketts
First Brigade Brig. Gen. Abram Duryea
97th New York • 104th New York • 105th New York • 107th Pennsylvania

Second Brigade Brig. Gen. Zealous B. Tower
26th New York • 94th New York • 88th Pennsylvania • 90th Pennsylvania

Third Brigade Col. John W. Stiles
12th Massachusetts • 13th Massachusetts • 83rd New York (9th Militia)
11th Pennsylvania

Fourth Brigade Col. Joseph Thoburn
7th Indiana • 84th Pennsylvania • 110th Pennsylvania • 1st West Virginia

Artillery
2nd Maine Light Artillery • 5th Maine Light Artillery
Battery F, 1st Pennsylvania Light Artillery • Battery C, Pennsylvania Light Artillery

Cavalry Brigade (Temporarily attached) Brig. Gen. George D. Bayard
1st Maine • 2nd New York • 1st New Jersey • 1st Pennsylvania
1st Rhode Island

PENNSYLVANIA RESERVES Brig. Gen. John F. Reynolds
First Brigade Brig. Gen. George G. Meade
3rd Pennsylvania Reserves • 4th Pennsylvania Reserves
7th Pennsylvania Reserves • 8th Pennsylvania Reserves
13th Pennsylvania Reserves (1st Rifles)

Second Brigade Brig. Gen. Truman Seymour
1st Pennsylvania Reserves • 2nd Pennsylvania Reserves
5th Pennsylvania Reserves • 6th Pennsylvania Reserves

Third Brigade Brig. Gen. Conrad F. Jackson
9th Pennsylvania Reserves • 10th Pennsylvania Reserves
11th Pennsylvania Reserves • 12th Pennsylvania Reserves

Artillery Capt. Dunbar R. Ransom
Battery A, 1st Pennsylvania Light Artillery
Battery B, 1st Pennsylvania Light Artillery
Battery G, 1st Pennsylvania Light Artillery • Battery C, 5th U.S. Artillery

Suggested Reading

THE BATTLE OF SECOND MANASSAS

Injustice on Trial: Second Bull Run, General Fitz John Porter's Court-Martial, and the Schofield Board Investigation That Restored His Good Name
Curt Anders
Curt Anders Books LLC, 2002
ISBN: 978-1578601103

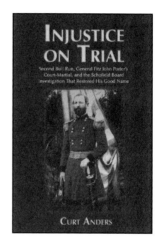

An early historical investigation into the historiography of V Corps commander Porter's court-martial and retrial. It is a great starting point to understanding the fallout of Porter's actions at Second Manassas and Pope's wayward accusations against the Army of the Potomac general.

The Military Memoirs of General John Pope
Peter Cozzens and Robert I. Girardi, eds.
The University of North Carolina Press, 2010
ISBN: 978-0-8078-6524-8

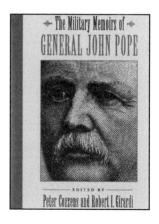

John Pope spared no ink in the post war years reasoning, justifying, explaining, and blaming others for his actions and decisions during the Second Manassas campaign, particularly the events of August 29-30, 1862. Between 1886 and 1891, Pope wrote 29 articles in a series for the *National Tribune* detailing all of his war experiences. The editors have compiled and annotated these pieces into this single volume. To understand the war through Pope's eyes, this is an essential volume.

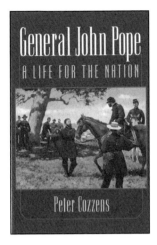

General John Pope: A Life for the Nation
Peter Cozzens
University of Illinois Press, 2000
ISBN: 978-0252023637

Cozzens, known for his seminal Western Theater studies and many other contributions to Civil War scholarship, presents a balanced biography of the Union general from early life through his post Second Manassas army career. The author reveals an illustrious army career in both the concluding war years and into the 1870s with many contributions still felt by the United States military today.

Confederate Tide Rising: Robert E. Lee and the Making of Southern Strategy, 1861–1862
Joseph L. Harsh
The Kent State University Press, 1998
ISBN: 978-0873385800

The author, known as one the most prominent scholars of the Confederate army in the Maryland campaign, published the book as a prequel to his larger study. The work seeks to explain military decisions made by Confederate President Jefferson Davis and Gen. Robert E. Lee that ultimately led to the battle of Antietam. The chapters that focus on July and August 1862 are essential reading to understanding Confederate strategy, or lack thereof, during the Second Manassas campaign.

Return to Bull Run: The Campaign and Battle of Second Manassas
by John J. Hennessy
University of Oklahoma Press, 1999
ISBN: 978-0806131870

The definitive campaign and battle study on Second Manassas. First published in the late 1980s, this single volume work has withstood the test of time. Its use of primary sources to inform both the narrative and interpretation of events in August 1862 is second to none. Although daunting to some at nearly 500 pages, it is essential reading to anyone wishing to understand this important moment during the American Civil War.

Second Manassas Battlefield Map Study
John Hennessy
Lynchburg: Howard, 1985
ISBN: 978-1561900091

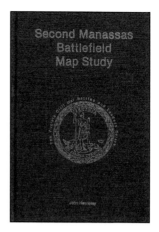

The author produced a set of 16 maps that detailed the battle in great depth, showing regimental through division level actions. This work was meant to accompany the maps. Each several hour segment reflected on the maps is covered in the map study using many primary sources and concise analysis.

Second Manassas: Longstreet's Attack and the Struggle for Chinn Ridge
Scott C. Patchan
Potomac Books, 2011
ISBN: 978-1597976879

Longstreet's massive August 30 assault against John Pope's left flank swept the Federal army from the field. Patchan, a historian with numerous published works on Eastern Theater engagements, devotes the entirety of this work to this attack. A great tactical study, the walking tour at its conclusion provides readers the opportunity to walk in the footsteps of the attack.

Radical Sacrifice: The Rise and Ruin of Fitz John Porter
William Marvel
The University of North Carolina Press, 2021
ISBN: 978-1469661858

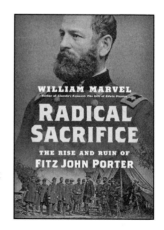

Marvel has written the newest, and perhaps definitive, biography of this Federal officer. His painstaking research and detailed accounting of Second Manassas's biggest officer casualty is balanced and engaging. A deeper look into the political machinations behind Pope's accusations that led to Porter's dismissal and long road to redemption is the true genius of the narrative.

About the Authors

Dan Welch is a Park Ranger at Gettysburg National Military Park. Author of several books on the American Civil War, Dan is also the editor of the long-running *Gettysburg Magazine*, the Emerging Revolutionary War Series, and co-editor of several volumes in the Emerging Civil War's 10th Anniversary Series. A historian at Emerging Civil War for over eight years, he has also published numerous essays, articles, and book reviews.

Kevin R. Pawlak is a historic site manager for Prince William County's Office of Historic Preservation and a Certified Battlefield Guide at Antietam National Battlefield. He previously worked as a Park Ranger at Harpers Ferry National Historical Park. This is Kevin's seventh book about the American Civil War, including *To Hazard All: A Guide to the Maryland Campaign, 1862*, part of the Emerging Civil War Series.